Praise for
Deacons in Today's Black Baptist Church

"Dr. Marvin McMickle challenges church leaders to look with fresh eyes at the office of deacon. Although this work is structured in the context of today's black Baptist church, it will be an invaluable resource for all Baptist churches. Dr. McMickle places the office of the deacon back into an appropriate biblical framework, while providing insight for selecting and training deacons for the twenty-first century. Rather than avoid much debated issues like women deacons, he faces them head on. It is a must read!"

—Rev. Kasey D. Jones, Senior Pastor,
National Baptist Memorial Church, Washington, DC

"The primary audience for this book is the local congregation, and it will also be a welcome resource for seminary classrooms where students are preparing for ministry. Seminarians reading this book will be led to consider new ways to envision the roles and responsibilities of deacons."

—Rev. Dr. Marsha Brown Woodard, Instructor in Christian Ministry, Palmer Theological Seminary, Wynnewood, PA; Transitional Minister, First Baptist Church, Wayne, PA

"Dr. McMickle speaks to the black Baptist church in a relevant, timely manner. The book is well-written, purposeful, and pertinent to the church today. Personally, I feel the book can be applied to the church at large, not just black Baptist congregations. I highly recommend."

—Book Bargains & Previews

"An excellent and timely text for the men and women who provide leadership in their churches. It is full of useful suggestions that provide important information in helping the church and ministry to grow and flourish."

—BlackandChristian.com

"*Deacons in Today's Black Baptist Church* informs, inspires, encourages, and challenges deacons of any race. It is obvious the author knows his audience well for he does not dodge controversial issues but rather walks into them with faith, courage, boldness, and biblical and historical evidence."

—Edward Hammett, Deacon Consultant & Author of *Reaching People Under 40 While Keeping People Over 60*, thecolumbiapartnership.org

"Many readers will appreciate how McMickle addresses several hot-button issues with a straightforward and scholarly yet gentle approach that is too often absent in the life of Baptist congregations. All Baptists could benefit from reading his two chapters that discuss women in ministry, and by extension sexism, in congregational life."

—*Baptist Studies Bulletin*, September 2010

Deacons in Today's Black Baptist Church

MARVIN A. McMICKLE

FOREWORD BY JULIUS R. SCRUGGS

JUDSON PRESS
PUBLISHERS SINCE 1824
VALLEY FORGE, PA

Judson Press has made every effort to trace the ownership of all quotes. In the
event of a question arising from the use of a quote, we regret any error made
and will be pleased to make the necessary correction in future printings and
editions of this book.

Most Bible quotations in this volume are from the New Revised Standard
Version of the Bible (NRSV), copyright © 1989 by the Division of Christian
Education of the National Council of the Churches of Christ in the United
States of America. Used by permission. All rights reserved.

Other Scripture versions are marked as follows:
The Holy Bible, King James Version (KJV)
The HOLY BIBLE: *New International Version,* copyright © 1973, 1978, 1984.
Used by permission of Zondervan Bible Publishers. (NIV)
The New King James Version. Copyright © 1972, 1984 by Thomas Nelson
Inc. (NKJV)
The Today's English Version - Second Edition © 1992 by American Bible
Society. Used by permission. (TEV)
The HOLY BIBLE, Today's New International Version™ TNIV.® Copyright
© 2001, 2005 by Biblica, Inc.™ Used by permission of Zondervan. All rights
reserved worldwide. www.zondervan.com. (TNIV)

Interior design by Jeanne Williams.
Cover art by Dane Tilghman.
Cover design by Tobias Becker and Birdbox Graphic Design (www.birdbox-
design.com.)

Library of Congress Cataloging-in-Publication Data

McMickle, Marvin Andrew.
  Deacons in today's Black Baptist church / Marvin A. McMickle ; foreword
by Julius R. Scruggs.
    p. cm.
  ISBN 978-0-8170-1640-1 (pbk. : alk. paper) 1. African American Baptists.
2. Deacons--Baptists. I. Title.
  BX6448.M39 2010
  262'.15608996073--dc22
                                          2010010540

Printed in the U.S.A.
First Edition, 2010.

Contents

Foreword   vii

Acknowledgements   ix

Introduction   xi

1. What Does the Bible Say about Deacons?   1

2. The Office of the Deacon in 1 Timothy 3:8-13   24

3. Deacons in the Black Baptist Church   35

4. Training for Deacons in Today's Black Church   56

5. In the Footsteps of Phoebe: Women Deacons   76
   in the Black Baptist Church

6. How One Church Embraced Women   91
   in Ordained Ministry

7. A Twenty-first Century Look at a First   102
   Century Ministry

8. Profiles in Service   116

Appendix A: Questionnaire about the Role of   135
   Deacons in the Black Baptist Church

Appendix B: Results of the Questionnaire about the   138
   Role of Deacons in the Black Baptist Church

Foreword

Among the leadership ministries that God has ordained within the Christian church are the ministries of the pastor and deacon. Explaining that leadership capacity is clearly determined by the capacity to serve, Jesus said, "Whoever wants to be first must be last of all and servant of all" (Mark 9:35).

The pastoral and diaconate (deacons) ministries have existed for centuries. The ministry of the pastor is first mentioned in the Old Testament book of Jeremiah (see Jeremiah 17:16, KJV), and the ministry of the deacon is first referenced in the earliest days of the New Testament church (see Acts 6). However, in more recent years, a regrettable and unnecessary tension has arisen in some circles regarding the deacon's role and scope of authority, particularly as it relates to the ministry and authority of the pastor. Such tension is often rooted in a simple misunderstanding of the respective biblical roles and functions of pastor and deacon.

In this insightful book, Rev. Dr. Marvin A. McMickle uses linguistic study and a sound hermeneutic to present a solid examination of the biblical origins of the office of the deacon. His biblically-based premise is that deacons are called to minister to the spiritual and benevolence needs of the congregation, working as servants and helpers in partnership with the pastor, who is assigned to lead or shepherd the church. This understanding of the deacon's role gives clarity to questions about how the local church is to be governed and how the needs of its people are to be met.

Dr. McMickle's book does more than explore the biblical role of the deacon. This practical resource also offers an invaluable training model for trial deacons, a model that is particularly relevant for Baptist congregations in the African American context. Additionally, the book addresses the often-debated issue of the place of women in the diaconate and other ministries, acknowledging ultimately that questions surrounding such issues are usually best resolved at the level of the local church.

Deacons in Today's Black Baptist Church is a gem mined from sound biblical truth and crisp theological understanding, polished by the practical experiences and insights gleaned from the author's more than three decades of pastoral ministry. My prayer is that every reader will find this text to be a helpful and balanced resource for local church ministry.

Rev. Dr. Julius R. Scruggs
President
National Baptist Convention, USA, Incorporated

Acknowledgments

The fact that this book has come to publication is the result of significant contributions of time and thought from persons across this country. I want to thank all my clergy colleagues from United Pastors in Mission in Greater Cleveland, Ohio, for being the first group to take the survey that provided data on how the ministry of deacons functions in today's churches. I am deeply grateful to the late Dr. Thurman Walker of San Antonio, Texas, for providing me with an opportunity to survey a group of pastors in a different part of the country to discover what difference, if any, might exist concerning the role of deacons from one region of the nation to another. I also want to thank the other pastors randomly chosen from cities and regions all across the United States whose input and counsel were invaluable to the preparation of this book.

I owe a special word of thanks to Dr. Julius Scruggs, the esteemed pastor of the First Missionary Baptist Church of Huntsville, Alabama, and current president of the National Baptist Convention USA, Inc. We found ourselves together at a Martin Luther King Jr. event in Huntsville, and out of that single encounter, Dr. Scruggs was willing to read the book in its earliest form and write the foreword that is now a part of the finished project. Given the enormous demands of his schedule, I am eternally grateful that he was willing to make time to play such a crucial role in the development of this project. He is a pastor and a president extraordinaire, and I cherish both his friendship and his good counsel!

I, along with all Judson Press authors, am indebted to the ever-vigilant Rebecca Irwin-Diehl. As editor of Judson Press, she not only works to determine which books will be published, but she also works alongside the authors to make sure that each Judson book is as good as it can possibly be. We began talking about this project at a session of the Samuel DeWitt Proctor Conference in 2007. From that time until the book was finished, we worked together to shape the book, narrow the focus, clarify the central argument, and even select the cover art. We are both aware that the cover art does not bear the image of any female deacons. However, we very much wanted to celebrate the artistic genius of Dane Tilghman, a local artist in the Philadelphia area, hoping that the content of the book would clarify what our position really is as it concerns women deacons in the black Baptist church.

The time it takes to research and write a book usually comes at the expense of someone central to the life of the author. In my case, it is my beloved wife, Peggy, to whom I have been joyously married since 1975. She supports me in my ministry of writing, and without that support none of the work I have done in this, my thirteenth book, would have been possible.

Thanks also go out to the members of Antioch Baptist Church and to the president and academic dean at Ashland Theological Seminary (Ohio). In both instances, they allow me the time it takes to make research and writing a central part of my vocation. I am indebted to them for their support, and I hope the finished product is deserving of the time and trust they have granted me to bring this book to completion.

Introduction

What is a deacon? Someone whose principle task is to provide benevolent support for members of the congregation in their times of special need? Someone who plays a "leading" role in attending all worship, study, and fellowship events in the life of the congregation? Someone who by word and deed models and demonstrates the fruits of the spirit as listed in Galatians 5:22-23 as that person interacts with the pastor and with members of the congregation?

Or is the deacon someone who seeks primarily to exercise an oversight role where the activities of the pastor and the general administration of the church are concerned? Many boards of deacons seem to view themselves as a board of directors who meet to approve programs and establish policies. This seems to be the case even if the majority of the members of that board do not attend one night of the church's annual revival service, or one day of Vacation Bible School, and even if they seldom attend a funeral service—not even for long-standing and active members of the congregation.

This lack of clarity about the appropriate roles and responsibilities of deacons can result in tensions and conflicts that can have a negative effect on the congregation in which they are serving. When deacons see themselves as being there to serve the spiritual and benevolent needs of the congregation, and when they see themselves as fulfilling that role in partnership with the pastor of that congregation there should be no problem. On the other hand, when deacons set aside their role as servants of the church and adopt instead the role of supervisor or "boss of the pastor" the stage is being set for a power struggle that has the potential of diverting the entire congregation away from the work of ministry that should be its primary focus.

Our understanding of the role and responsibilities of the deacon in the Baptist church in general, and in the black Baptist church in particular, has come to a critical crossroad. Enough contentious business meetings have been held, the tone of which could have been avoided if there had been in that meeting a clear understanding on the part of everyone present as to the precise role of deacons in the Baptist church. Enough congregations have become divided, enough pastors have been dismissed or chosen to resign, and enough deacons have been removed from their positions as a result of there not being an agreed upon view in those churches of what is the role and work of deacons in that church.

Corporate Models and Baptist Church Dynamics

Many deacons and other lay leaders in Baptist churches generally and black Baptist churches in particular come to their understanding of their role by looking at how relationships work in the secular work setting. Relationships between employers and employees, supervisors and policy-makers on the job get carried over into our understandings of how the church should operate. When the governance structures and work-place relationships are imported from secular institutions into the life of the church, there comes the belief that the pastor is "the employee" of the congregation rather than its spiritual and operational leader, and that the deacons' chief responsibility is to oversee and supervise all pastoral activities and initiatives.

People who hold jobs such as school principal or administrator, department manager, section leader, or corporate executive will spend every day of their working lives navigating the territory of power and position, mindful of who is accountable and answerable to whom. When that same person becomes a member of the church deacon board, they are inclined to bring with them that same corporate mentality. The question is whether that corporate approach is useful or appropriate when it comes to church governance in general and to the relationship between pastors and deacons in particular.

Not surprisingly, as more and more African Americans move into positions of ownership, supervision, and authority on the job, much of that ethos of corporate organizational life filters into the understanding of the roles they may play in the life of their churches. Using such a corporate model, today's deacons may approach the role as one of oversight, accountability, and even approval in relation to pastoral decisions and initiative. A key purpose of this book is to consider the role of the deacon as it was formulated in Scripture and as it has evolved in history, and thus determine the most appropriate and advantageous relationship between deacon and pastor and between deacon and congregation. What does the ministry of deacons entail? How should the church identify candidates for deacon? What qualities are required or recommended for a deacon? What was the biblical purpose for the office of the deacon? How has the historical context of being black and Baptist in America influenced the evolution of that office? How do we fulfill the scriptural purposes of a deacon ministry in our local black Baptist churches today? These are among the questions this book will seek to address.

Chapter 1 will trace the office of deacon to its origins in Acts 6:1-7. It will show the Greek word for deacon is used in a verb form to suggest an action that should be taken and not a noun form that would suggest a position to be assumed or a title to be held. More importantly, that position will be shown to be one of service rendered and not supervision over the service of others. Chapter 1 will also seek to point out the relationship between the first deacons and the original twelve apostles who ordained the deacons and assigned them to their position. That will lay the foundation for how pastors and deacons should work together today.

In Chapter 2 attention will be given to 1 Timothy 3:8-13, which is the other biblical passage that offers an in-depth look at the role and responsibilities of the deacon. When considered alongside Acts 6:1-7, this passage establishes the deacon as one of only two offices in the church with roots in the Bible (the second office being the preacher or pastor). These two passages not only describe the qualities and characteristics desirable for anyone who is named to become a deacon, but they also describe a working relationship that can safeguard against the influence of corporate models or cultural traditions serving as the basis for deciding on the duties of the deacon.

In Chapter 3 the focus will be on how the role of the deacon has evolved from its biblical origins to how it is understood and practiced in today's Baptist church in general and in the black Baptist church in particular.

Chapter 4 will suggest essential components of a training program for prospective deacons. Such a program could also be used as the basis for a continuing education for persons already serving as deacons in local churches. This chapter is not intended to set out a required curriculum for use in every church. Rather, it offers broad areas of activity and responsibility of which every new deacon should be made aware, including the ordination or installation process by which a trial deacon is established as a full member of the board of deacons. It will also urge local churches to be sure to introduce new deacons to any expectations about the office that may be unique to that particular, autonomous Baptist congregation.

Chapter 5 will break new ground concerning the role of deacons in the black Baptist church. It will consider what the Bible does and does not say about women serving as deacons, giving attention to 1 Timothy 2:11-12 and 1 Corinthians 14:33-35 to determine if Paul's injunctions concerning women's roles in the first-century church should be maintained in today's black

Baptist church. Attention will also be given to Romans 16:1-2, where Paul refers to Phoebe using the title *diakonos*.

Chapter 6 offers a detailed look at how one black Baptist church came to the decision to ordain women as deacons. It will also point out some of the consequences that can result when churches do proceed with choosing women to serve in this position, especially as it concerns interchurch fellowship.

Chapter 7 focuses on insights gleaned from a nationwide survey that was conducted as part of this study to determine how the work of the deacon is understood in 44 congregations across the country. These survey results will offer a fairly clear glimpse into the work of deacons in the twenty-first century black Baptist church.

Finally, Chapter 8 provides a series of profiles of deacons of various ages, from various churches, and with diverse life experiences. Through their voices and perceptions we will gain added insight into the roles and responsibilities of deacons in today's black Baptist church.

•Chapter 1•
What Does the Bible Say about Deacons?

In my nearly forty years of pastoral ministry, I have watched many black Baptist churches struggle with questions regarding the role and responsibilities of the deacon. I have heard clergy colleagues vent about the "devilish deacons" who call themselves spiritual leaders but position themselves as adversaries of the pastor, are regularly absent from worship service, never show up at Bible study, rarely visit the sick, and show no interest in the spiritual lives or practical needs of the congregation. Of course, I have also observed pastors who use their deacons as little more than personal assistants or glorified gofers, exploiting the humble heart of God's servants for their own convenience or luxury. Surely the answer to the question of what it means to be deacon is both less and more than these extreme examples.

The goal of this book is to present a clear scriptural understanding of the role and responsibilities of deacons in the black Baptist church. It is essential for both pastors and deacons to share a biblically rooted understanding of what it means to be a deacon. One reason I believe this biblical emphasis is so important is because I recognize whatever observations I might make about the role of the deacon might easily be interpreted as biased toward my own self-interests as a pastor or those of my colleagues in pastoral ministry. Of course, it is equally true that deacons who write about the work of the deacon could similarly be challenged for possible biases in favor of whatever outcome might best suit them.

Surely, pastors, deacons, and many others in the church will have strong feelings and opinions about the role and responsibilities of the deacon. In the end, however, no perspective on the role of the deacon can be taken as authoritative if it is based upon nothing more than personal convictions or anecdotal evidence. Nor can any argument be adopted if it simply seeks to strengthen, without any qualifications, existing views concerning the office of deacon in Baptist churches. An authoritative understanding of the role and responsibilities of a deacon must be rooted in the Scriptures rather than in what any particular pastor or deacon may think or believe.

If the Bible is going to serve as the ultimate authority in this discussion, then the first question is fairly obvious: *What does the Bible say about the role and responsibilities of the deacon?* In this chapter we will make a determined effort to offer an unbiased, impartial, and objective assessment of Acts 6:1-7, which is one of the two primary New Testament passages that address both the creation of the office of the deacon as well as what is expected in the performance of that office. Later in the book, we will look at the biblical material addressing two other related questions: *Who can serve as a deacon?* and *How should deacons relate to those who serve in the clergy?* We'll also take some time to consider what the Scriptures have to say about whether it is appropriate for women to serve as deacons.

Training Begins with the Bible

Let me state from the outset that while I believe familiarity with the biblical material is absolutely essential in preparing deacons for their work, it alone is not enough. The training any local church provides for its deacons will necessarily include additional information about the duties of deacons within that particular congregation. Given the autonomy of each Baptist church, the specific tasks performed by deacons will vary from one congregation to another. Churches will have differing expectations about the role of deacons regarding the Lord's Supper, baptism, midweek services, leading devotional services, visiting the sick, overseeing the benevolence arm of the church, and other tasks. Thus, it is important that persons who serve as deacons receive some instruction in what that role entails in that particular congregation.

Churches training new deacons would also be wise to include some input from the voices of experience. Those who have served as deacons for many years should be allowed an opportunity to offer their insights to newer members of the board concerning the roles and responsibilities of this office. In addition, there are many fine books on the work of the deacon in the Baptist church that can be used as part of a training process before deacons begin their duties in this important church position.[1]

None of that training, however, is an adequate alternative to what is being suggested here. The office of the deacon is a biblical office, and as such it is absolutely essential that attention be given first and foremost to what the Bible has to say about it. That is the best way to break both the corporate model and the patterns of inherited church tradition that seem to have a lock on how the role and responsibilities of the deacon are understood by many who hold that office.

An Ordained Position

There are many leadership positions in the Baptist church that are both essential and deserving of respect and recognition. Trustees serve in response to the demands of the state and by vote of the congregation. A myriad of staff members ranging from musicians, to office personnel, to groundskeepers and security guards may be employed by the church to provide service in accordance with a specific job description as defined by the congregation.

Nonetheless, one thing sets preachers and deacons apart from all other leaders in the church, especially in the Baptist church. These two positions—preacher and deacon—are the only two offices whose creation is traceable directly to the Bible. The need for preachers and deacons was not invented by a church council or denominational tribunal, nor was it the result of changes in the culture over the years. Preachers and deacons are offices established within the biblical text itself.

The Bible makes it clear that preachers and deacons are set apart from all other leaders in the church by the solemn and ancient practice of ordination, also known as "the laying on of hands." (Deacon is the only church office other than pastor that traditionally involves ordination.) This is why any attempt to understand how deacons should function within the context of a black Baptist church cannot begin or end with matters of Baptist polity. Nor can such a discussion begin or end with the cultural norms and values found within any given black community at any given point in time. The discussion about the role and responsibilities of a deacon must begin with serious consideration of the biblical passages most closely associated with the creation of that office.

The emphasis on Scripture is a given when it come to ordaining new pastors. The ordination council for a Baptist preacher would never consider proceeding with its work without being sure the candidate had been exposed to all the relevant biblical passages dealing with the roles and responsibilities of the ordained clergy. I cannot remember a single instance in my nearly four decades of participating in clergy ordination councils when the candidate was not asked about the importance of the call stories of Moses (Exodus 3), Amos (Amos 6), or Ezekiel (Ezekiel 3); the story of Jesus speaking in the synagogue in Nazareth (Luke 4), or Paul's words in 2 Timothy 4:1-8 that speak to the work of preaching the gospel. In the same way, it is equally important that adequate attention be given to the relevant biblical passages that relate to the creation of the position of deacon in the church.

Acts 6 and the First Deacons

There are two biblical passages that provide the clearest and most commonly agreed upon information about the creation of the position of deacon: Acts 6:1-7 and 1 Timothy 3:8-13. In this chapter, we will focus on the passage from Acts 6, because it is here that the apostles first recognized the need for a ministry that would become known as the deacons' ministry. In this story of origins, we will find the clues needed to develop an understanding of what it means to be a deacon. (Later, in chapter 2, we will turn our attention to 1 Timothy 3 for its insights on how to answer the question *Who is qualified to be a deacon?*)

Interestingly, while the Greek word *diakonous* (which we translate into the English word *deacon*) appears prominently in the 1 Timothy 3 passage, this word does not appear in the passage in Acts 6; at least not in the form of a noun that would point to a specific office. Nevertheless, the Greek word *diakonia* appears in Acts 6:1, and the word *diakonein* appears in Acts 6:2. Taken together these two verses and word usages suggest *an action* to be taken rather than *an office or position* to be filled. In other words Acts 6 begins with a focus on a specific service that needs to be done, and then turns its attention to the qualifications of the persons who should be assigned that task.

This is no small point. If Baptist churches seeking to understand the role and responsibilities of the deacon begin with "the office," then they may quickly end up with people seeking to fill a position that has become associated with a certain degree of authority and influence. If, on the other hand, we start the discussion as Acts 6 does—with the need that existed and "the service" to be offered to the community—then the discussion moves in an entirely different direction. "What can I do for you?" takes the place of "This is what I expect you to do." Right from the very start, Acts 6 places the focus on a service that needs to be accomplished rather than on a position of power that needs to be filled.

Who Will Serve the Needy?

This passage from Acts points to a specific set of circumstances in the life of the early Christian church in Jerusalem, as well as to the proposed solution. An administrative problem had emerged, and the twelve apostles conceived of a response that began to lay the foundation for what would eventually become the office of the deacon. Certain widows were not receiving their fair allotment from the communal resources of that church. When a complaint about that inequity was brought to the attention of the twelve apostles, they were reluctant to enter any further into that aspect of the life and work of the church. The apostles were concerned that any time they devoted to "waiting on tables" (their term for serving those in need in this way) would take away from the time they needed to invest in their ministry of preaching and prayer (Acts 6:4). The twelve apostles set up a process by which seven individuals were selected by the community of believers, brought to the twelve apostles for consecration, and then placed in charge of this specific responsibility. Acts 6:1-7 lists the qualifications demanded of those seven people and sets forth their job description.

Even though it is common for Baptist congregations to read this passage when new deacons are ordained, and even though deacons may turn to this passage in an attempt to better understand their role, I do not think we have really paid enough attention to what is going on here. Sadly, most of the problems associated with deacons in the Baptist church are directly related to a failure to understand the situation in Acts 6:1-7. How many church fights and feuds could have been avoided if people paid closer attention to what is really being discussed here?

The Impact of Pentecost

The need for deacons or servants in the Jerusalem church that is discussed in Acts 6 can be traced to the impact of Pentecost as reported in Acts 2. Originally, Pentecost was a Jewish festival occurring fifty days after Passover. It was a celebration of the harvest when life-giving crops were gathered up all across the country. It was an important observance for an agrarian society. The first Christian Day of Pentecost fell on the day of this Jewish festival. This transformed version of that day marks the beginning of the Christian church and lays special emphasis on the great harvest of 3000 converts added to the church that day. Just as Jesus had altered and transformed the Passover meal to now represent the Lord's Supper, so the early Christian church altered and transformed Pentecost to represent the birth and growth of the Christian church.

The rapid expansion of the Christian community on its very first day brought both blessings and challenges to the early church in Jerusalem. Obviously, the good news was the large number of people who became Christians in response to Peter's preaching and the outpouring of the Holy Spirit. However, that stunning growth brought with it greater racial and cultural diversity—challenges the church continues to wrestle with to this very day.

The Acts account indicates that the people who responded to Peter's sermon came from every nation, language, and culture both in the Mediterranean region and beyond. Some of the new Christian converts had come to Jerusalem to observe this major Jewish holiday in the holy city, while others were residents of the city. Normally, pilgrims who journeyed to Jerusalem would return home after a festival, and those who lived in that city would get on with their lives without any substantial changes having occurred. Obviously that was not the case with this particular observance of Pentecost. This time many of those pilgrims remained, joining the residents of the multicultural city of Jerusalem as part of this new movement that would soon be called Christianity (Acts 11:26).

The expansion of this new movement brought new problems of organization and structure. According to Acts 4:32-35 the early church was organized around a communal structure. The members of that Christian community sold or donated their earthly possessions and then pooled their collective wealth— no one held private property. The community's funds were entrusted to the twelve apostles who were called upon to dis- tribute them to members of the community "as any had need" (Acts 4:35).

Almost from the start the apostles found themselves serving in a dual capacity. On the one hand they exercised spiritual leadership over the community, primarily through their preach- ing and teaching. But they were also called on to meet the physical needs of the members of this community that held all things in common. That part of their work was exercised largely through their supervision and distribution of resources to those in need. This second responsibility of the twelve apostles would lay the groundwork for what would eventually become the office of the deacon.

Spiritual Leaders and Acts of Benevolence

Judaism had a long practice of providing for the physical as well as the spiritual needs of the community, especially those who were considered poor and needy. Ernst Haenchen notes that first-century Judaism practiced two kinds of relief for the poor. Each Friday those residents of the local community who were poor were given enough money for fourteen meals. Strangers—those whose presence there was transitory—were given daily offerings of food and drink. The money distributed was provided by the Jewish community through donations made at the temple or the synagogue, as well as through door- to-door solicitations performed by local officials.[2]

Thus, an arrangement whereby the local Christian commu- nity would aid its neediest members through a system of com- munal self-care was by no means unique. Judaism had been doing that for centuries. So it is not surprising that a similar practice was among the first things established by the early Christian community in Jerusalem. C.S.C. Williams observes that providing for the needs of the impoverished within the Jerusalem church became a main feature of the ministry of Paul who had to "beg money from his Gentile converts." Williams also hints that one argument Paul used to raise this money was to encourage these new Christians to "exceed the righteousness of the Jews."[3] ⎯⎯⎯⎯⎯

In light of Judaism's long history of spiritual leaders overseeing the collection and distribution of resources to the needy, it was natural that the concern that arises in Acts 6 would be brought to the attention of the twelve apostles. They were clearly the spiritual leaders of that community, and it was understood that this was their problem to resolve. The action they took was not unlike the system set up within Judaism: the spiritual leaders embraced the importance of the task but delegated responsibility for its oversight to others. The High Priest of Israel did not oversee the weekly or daily distribution of resources to the needy in his community; he just made sure this ministry took place. Similarly, the twelve apostles did not personally oversee the problem brought before them; they created a system of oversight to make sure that work was accomplished. This is how the office of the deacon began.

The Challenge of Diversity

Given Judaism's long history of providing for the physical needs of community members, and the similarity of the plan adopted by the early Christian church, what led to this new complaint about the way resources were being distributed within the Jerusalem church? Acts 6 traces the problem directly to the increased ethnic and cultural diversity that accompanied the stunning growth of the early church. That diversity seems to have resulted in some perceived bias or discrimination in the distribution of the commonly held resources. The widows of the Greek-speaking Jews who had become Christians were receiving less than the widows of the Hebrew-speaking converts to the faith.

The text says the Greek-speaking widows "complained." This word recalls the time of the Exodus when the Hebrews "complained" or grumbled or murmured about their lack of food and water during that journey. This comparison suggests that, as with the Hebrews during the Exodus, the problem faced by the Greek-speaking widows was persistent and increasingly frustrating. Their sense of feeling ignored and overlooked eventually boiled over into their complaint to the twelve apostles.

The problem for the early church in Jerusalem was both subtle and blatant, as is the case with all forms of discrimination. All the widows involved had been married to Jewish men who had converted to Christianity. However, their shared membership in the family of faith was not enough to trump the linguistic and ethnic differences that separated them.

These early Christians were operating with a keen awareness of the Mosaic Law that demanded care and provision for widows, as made clear in passages such as Deuteronomy 14:29, 16:11, 24:19, 26:12, and 27:19—all of which mandated that special care be given to widows, orphans, and foreigners. Caring for the widows was something that these Jewish converts to Christianity would readily understand. The book of Ruth was a reminder of the widows' unrestricted right to glean the fields for food (Ruth 2:1-2) as well as of the provision that a widow be taken into the home of the nearest male relative after her husband died (Ruth 4:5-10).

Nevertheless, the early Christians' faithful adherence to this ancient Jewish practice, as well as their adherence to the daily and weekly care of the needy discussed earlier, was directly challenged by forces with equally ancient origins: racism, nationalism, and ethnic rivalries. The widows of Hebrew-speaking Christian converts were being cared for, but their Greek-speaking counterparts were not. The spirit of benevolence and the spirit of bias in the distribution of that benevolence have equally deep roots in the Christian church.

The bias that divided first-century Christians has not left the church of the twenty-first century. At least the members of the early church in Jerusalem all belonged to the same congregation, even if they received disparate treatment. Howard Thurman told of a Muslim man who attempted to visit The First Baptist Church in Roanoke, Virginia, in 1924. He was turned away and sent instead to the First Colored Baptist Church in that same city. The Muslim offered a mocking critique of the blatant racial bigotry among Christians: "Allah laughs aloud in his Mohammedan heaven when he sees the Christian spectacle: the First Baptist Church White, and the First Baptist Church Colored."[4] The words of Liston Pope that were oft-quoted by Martin Luther King Jr. remain true nearly 50 years after Pope spoke them: "The most racially segregated hour in America is 11:00 AM on Sunday morning."[5] It is clear that the racial divisions and ethnic biases that plague U.S. Christian churches today are in no sense unique or original; such divisions are as old as the original Christian church in Jerusalem.

A Proposed Solution

The twelve apostles were confronted with a situation that was, at the very least, an administrative problem. More likely, this unequal distribution of resource to Hebrew- and Greek-speaking widows marked the beginnings of some of the schisms that would divide the early church with reference to differences between what was required from Jewish and Greek converts to the faith. A similar issue can be seen in Acts 15 when the Jerusalem Council was convened by Paul and the twelve apostles to decide what aspects of Jewish law would be required of Gentile converts to Christianity.

This was the climate and context for the creation of a special office or position to assume the task of "waiting on tables"— which meant overseeing the fair distribution of the commonly held property. The instructions from the twelve apostles in Acts 6:3 were the following: "Select from among yourselves seven men of good standing, full of the Holy Spirit and wisdom, whom we may appoint to this task" (NRSV). That decision was agreed upon by everyone in the community, and seven individuals were identified and brought before the twelve apostles, who set them apart for their work through prayer and the laying on of hands. Those seven men assumed responsibility for the distribution of the commonly held property and especially for the unbiased care of all widows in need.

New Testament scholars point out the seven men chosen all had Greek names: Stephen, Philip, Procorus, Nicanor, Timon, Parmenas, and Nicolas. The community seemed to feel that selecting individuals who shared a cultural and linguistic bond with the widows who had been overlooked might minimize the chance of such oversights occurring again. Despite the fact that all seven men were Greek, they also possessed the necessary standing within the broader Jerusalem church. The fact that these men were consecrated to their new position clearly suggests the twelve apostles agreed with the multicultural community's decision.

Here is a lesson all multicultural and multi-lingual institutions should learn: Diversity within the membership necessitates diversity within the leadership. Within the Christian community, this practice actually began with Jesus, who selected his original twelve apostles from a wide array of political and vocational backgrounds. Among the apostles were both Simon the Zealot, an enemy of Rome, and Matthew the tax collector, an employee of Rome (Matthew 10:3-4). The inclusion of a Greek man named Philip proved to be strategic, as he was the apostle approached by a group of Greek Jews who were seeking an audience with Jesus (John 12:21). Needless to say, Paul was uniquely qualified to be the church's apostle to the Gentile world, given his strong training in Jewish law, his fluency in Greek, and his Roman citizenship.

Service Not Status

Robert Naylor points out, "The election of these seven qualified men is the real beginning of the deacon as a church officer."[6]

The Dictionary of Christianity in America picks up on this in writing about deacons in the early church:

> In the classical Greek, the term *diakonos* meant a servant, especially one who performed the menial task of waiting on tables. The evangelists adopted this term when they recorded Christ's description of his own ministry and that of his disciples, 'Whoever wants to become great among you must be your servant' (*diakonos*) (Mt. 20:26; Mk. 10:43). All Christian ministry, therefore, is to be diakonia.[7]

This entry from *The Dictionary of Christianity in America* continues by saying:

> Yet the church quite early began to designate official *diakonoi,* or servants, whose role was to look after the basic needs of the community, to carry messages, to purchase food for the poor and to prepare a place for the celebration of the Lord's Supper. Although the selection of seven men from the church of Jerusalem (Acts 6) was not the formal institution of the ordained diaconate, yet this episode is quite legitimately seen as an example of, and as a model for, the diaconate of special service.[8]

Acts 6 is a good place to begin a study of the roles and responsibilities of a deacon in the Baptist church, because this passage marks the beginning of the office of deacon in terms of service and not status.

Essential Characteristics of a Deacon

Acts 6:3 offers us the first listing of the qualities and character of those persons who should be assigned the task of "waiting on tables" or serving the needs of the church community. There are two clear criteria that seem to emerge: The people selected to fill this role were filled with the Holy Spirit and full of

wisdom. Some English translations point to a third possible criterion—individuals of good reputation or in good standing. All
of the versions of Acts 6 will use the words "seven men" meaning seven male members of the community. Given the context of
first-century Palestine it must be understood that women were
not and could not be chosen for this position. However, later
in this book the issue of women as deacons will be considered.
Here are several different translations of this important verse:[9]

> *Look ye out among you seven men of honest report, full of*
> *the Holy Spirit and wisdom.*
> (KJV)
> *Select from among yourselves seven men of good standing,*
> *full of the Spirit and of wisdom.*
> (NRSV)
> *Choose seven men from among you who are known to be*
> *full of the Spirit and wisdom.*
> (NIV)
> *Seek out from among you seven men of good reputation,*
> *full of the Holy Spirit and wisdom.*
> (NKJV)
> *Choose seven men among you who are known to be full of*
> *the Holy Spirit and wisdom.*
> (TEV)

Let us start by looking at each of the qualities that is mentioned in every English translation.

1. Full of the Holy Spirit

Surely the apostles were among those who were filled with the
Holy Spirit when the Christian church was born on Pentecost.
Therefore, it is not surprising that in looking to meet the need
in the Jerusalem church, they would seek people who also
showed some evidence of being touched by the transforming
work of the Holy Spirit. They were seeking individuals known
for their spiritual maturity and for their seasoned insight and

counsel—qualities that flow from their relationship with God and with the teachings of Christ.

In Acts 1:21-22, we find that when the apostles were looking for a replacement for Judas, the first criterion was someone who had been with Jesus from his baptism by John until his resurrection and ascension. They would not consider anyone who had not spent considerable time in the physical company of Jesus. When it came to the selection of the seven persons who would do the work of waiting on tables, the apostles kept to a similar standard of spiritual maturity and longevity in the community. This seems to be in keeping with the advice Paul gave in 1 Timothy 5:22: "Do not be hasty in the laying on of hands" (NIV).

2. Wisdom

The biblical world placed great stock in wisdom, which was not merely intelligence or understanding gained from worldly education or reading. When the twelve apostles instructed the people to choose seven men full of wisdom, using the Greek word *Sophia,* they were asking for people who possessed a level of understanding that God imparts to those who are close to God. Paul speaks in 1 Corinthians 2:6-7 of a wisdom that is hidden from the world but revealed to believers in Christ. In all likelihood, the core of that wisdom is the core of the gospel message: Jesus Christ is Lord. Nothing could undermine the strength of the church faster than spiritual leaders who lacked *wisdom,* who were not anchored in the teachings of the faith.

J. Oswald Sanders says:

> Wisdom is more than knowledge. . . . It involves the knowledge of God and the intricacies of the human heart. It is much more than knowledge; it is the right application of knowledge in moral and spiritual matters, in meeting baffling situations, and in the complexity of human

relationships. Knowing is gained by study, but when the Spirit fills a man, He imparts the wisdom to use and apply that knowledge correctly.[10]

3. Good Reputation

As we have mentioned, three of the five English translations examined mention an additional characteristic: The persons selected should be persons of good reputation, or good standing, in the community. Given the fact that the majority of translations include the matter of good reputation, it seems prudent to include that in the list of qualifications.

The apostles were seeking people widely known as good, upstanding members of the community. Given the issue of bias toward the widows of Grecian Jews in the church, it may have been especially important to select people widely known not to share in any such bias. Since the job would also involve the handling of the financial resources of the entire community, it would be important that those chosen be known for their honesty and trustworthiness. The matter of good standing or good reputation might also allow the community to search for people who were untainted by any views, values, or behaviors that might result in a lack of confidence in those persons when they assumed their duties.

Nothing would be worse for the church than if a deacon possessed a bad reputation as regards prejudices of any kind, mismanagement of church funds, inappropriate personal conduct, or any other actions that would discredit that person. It is difficult, if not impossible, for the church to relate properly to a spiritual leader who has been compromised by gossip, innuendo, and rumors concerning immorality or a general lack of personal integrity. Whenever someone is being considered to become a deacon, the church must consider whether that person possesses a good reputation both within the local church community and beyond.

However, New Testament scholar Mitzi Smith has pointed out that the phrase "good reputation" could also be translated as "witnesses."[11] This is interesting in light of what we have already said about the selection of an apostle to replace Judas that occurs in Acts 1:21. The individual selected to replace Judas as an apostle was to be "a witness with us of the resurrection." It is possible that the twelve apostles were looking for more than just someone with a reputation of honesty and integrity. They may have been looking for individuals who could bear an accurate witness to the teachings of the faith, a person whose testimony about Jesus and his teachings could be trusted.

This possibility that I am extracting from Smith's translation should not be overlooked. People in the church often ask deacons for their opinions about various aspects of the Christian faith in general, and of the Bible in particular. With that in mind, persons chosen to serve as deacons should be persons who can be trusted to offer a response that is faithful and true. When deacons do not have the answer to such questions themselves, they should be persons who can be trusted to seek out a fuller understanding from the pastor or another better-informed source and then report back what has been provided.

The Relationship between the Twelve and the Seven

This passage in Acts 6:1-7 is important for two other reasons. First, it sets forth the essential responsibilities of those who would fill the office that would come to be known as the deacon. Second, it sets forth the relationship between the twelve apostles and the seven men who were chosen. Before the word *deacon* was ever employed, Acts 6:1-7 instituted the task of "waiting on tables"—humble service to meet the physical needs of the poor without bias or discrimination. This text clearly demonstrates that authority in the church was already localized in the hands of the twelve apostles. There was no hint that the apostles were giving away that position of spiritual leadership. The issue for the deacons was primarily a matter of service to be given and not authority to be exercised.

The plan set forth in Acts 6:1-7 was to create a division of labor and responsibility within the church, not an agreement to share or shift power. The work of waiting on the tables would be assigned to the seven men chosen by the community but consecrated by the twelve apostles. The work of the seven was designed to relieve the twelve apostles of a specific task that had to be done, so that the apostles would not be drawn away from their chief responsibility—the ministry of the word (preaching) and prayer (most likely personal and intercessory prayer). Under this arrangement, two equally important and urgent areas of ministry could proceed simultaneously. The twelve apostles could devote themselves to areas of evangelism, church growth, and spiritual nurture and formation, while the seven deacons could proceed with benevolence and the day-to-day physical needs of the community.

Everyone Has a Unique Role

The twelve apostles and the seven men selected as deacons assumed their specific roles, and every indication is that the growth of the church continued unabated. Complaints about bias against Greek widows or preferential treatment toward Hebrew widows came to an immediate halt; there are no further reports of that being a problem within the Jerusalem church. The apostles' solution to this early church problem created the only other office requiring ordination or the laying on of hands: the deacon.

This pattern of the division of labor in accomplishing the work of the church was at work at many points in the life of the early Christian community. Growth came when different people fulfilled the roles assigned to them. There were tasks only Jesus could accomplish, and, thank God, he fulfilled God's plan for him. There were tasks assigned to Peter and John relative to the church in Jerusalem (Acts 3–4), which were vastly different from the assignments given to Paul during his three missionary journeys through Asia Minor (Acts 9–21). Paul asked the churches in Asia Minor to contribute to an offering that would support the struggling and oppressed Christian community back in Jerusalem (2 Corinthians 8:1–9:5). Specific work was expected from people like Barnabas, Timothy, Silas, and Demas. When these people performed the tasks assigned to them, the church prospered and Paul applauded their efforts. When they failed to perform their specific assignments, the church's ministry was impeded.

The early church was candid about how members' failing to fulfill their responsibilities affected the community and the advancement of the cause of Christ. Paul laments over the behavior of John Mark, whom Paul accused of failing to perform his duties in Pamphylia (Acts 15:36-40). This eventually led to a schism not only between Paul and John Mark, but also between Paul and Barnabas. Both then and now, schisms often occur in the church when leaders exceed or misunderstand the lengths and limits of their role and responsibility.

Paul also expressed grave disappointment when men like Demas, Crescens, and Titus failed to fulfill responsibilities assigned to them (2 Timothy 4:9-10). He reserved even more heated comments for Alexander the coppersmith, whom Paul accuses of having done him "a great deal of harm (2 Timothy 4:14-15). We are also reminded of Ananias and Sapphira who conspired to withhold money from the common resources after they had sold a piece of land (Acts 5:1-11). Just as the church in Macedonia was celebrated for its generosity (2 Corinthians 8:1-4), so were other members of the community criticized and even punished for their failure to perform duties expected of them. Those who serve as deacons must remember that the church runs best when each member fully performs the duties assigned to him or her. Trouble, schism, ill-will, and less effective ministry result when roles and responsibilities get confused.

T. Dewitt Smith's insights are helpful: "We generally hate anything that links us with servanthood; believing that such a role or action is beneath our self-perceived status."[12] We are overly influenced by a secular culture where the objective is to be promoted and to have others work under our oversight and authority. However, when it came to these seven men who were ordained by the twelve apostles, things work in exactly the opposite direction. By all appearances, these seven servants worked under the oversight and by the authority of the apostles.

What made this possible were the essential characteristics of the individuals selected: a good reputation, full of the Spirit and wisdom. T. DeWitt Smith writes:

> Such a combination would bring forth well-balanced men whose decisions would be made with the utmost care and caution. It would not be their attitude to seize power and influence and usurp the teaching patterns of the apostles, but to compliment [sic] the apostles by assisting them in unifying and harmonizing the church for effective Christian witness through service.[13]

Two Deacons Did More

While Acts 6:1-7 offers a clear division of roles and responsibilities between the twelve apostles and the seven individuals chosen to wait on tables, later chapters of Acts make it abundantly clear that the ministry of two of the seven selected as deacons was not limited just to the work of "waiting tables." Stephen and Philip were the first two recommended by the community to be brought before the twelve apostles for their approval and ordination. However, both of these servant deacons later moved beyond that role and became preachers and evangelists.

By Acts 7 Stephen was offering a full-blown defense of the Christian faith that results in his being stoned to death by those attempting to suppress any further talk about Jesus as Messiah. There is broad agreement that it was the deacon named Philip, rather than the apostle by the same name, who followed the example of Stephen and was the person chiefly responsible for the conversion and baptism of the Ethiopian

eunuch in Acts 8:26-39.[14] Thus, while all seven of the original deacons were called to wait on tables, and five of them
appear to have remained with that task, two of the seven
named in Acts 6:1-7 moved beyond that role into an evangelis-
tic ministry.

This is an important point, because there are many preachers and pastors serving in Baptist churches today who began
as deacons in a local church. Eventually, they confessed a call
and were ordained to the ministry of preaching, sometimes by
the same church that had earlier ordained them to be deacons.
While this move from one ordained position to another is not
a common occurrence in most black Baptist churches, it does
have ancient roots and a clear precedent. Stephen and Philip
would be among the earliest examples of deacons who later
moved into the ministry of declaring the Word.

As we consider the ministries of Stephen and Philip, we should
keep in mind the suggestion by Mitzi Smith that the "seven men of
good reputation" could be translated as seven men "having been
witnesses." Like the twelve apostles, Stephen and Philip seem to
have embraced the role of bearing witness to the faith. And like
the apostles, Stephen also suffered a martyr's death as a result
of bearing witness to the faith. This is not surprising since the
Greek word for *witness* is *marturia,* which has the same root as
the English word *martyr*.

The overwhelming majority of deacons will not make this
transition from one ordained position to another. However, it is
fairly clear that at least two of the seven original deacons called
and commissioned in Acts 6 did exactly that.

Why Was the Office of Deacon Created?

To summarize, Acts 6 reminds us that the work of deacons in
the church arose out of a specific need. The twelve apostles
realized they could not fulfill their own responsibilities of
preaching and prayer in the Jerusalem church if they had to
devote time to "waiting on tables" and to overseeing the fair

distribution of the communal property. Seven men known for their solid reputations within the community and their devout standing in relation to God and the church were to be selected by the people to take on this important work. The seven who were selected were brought to the apostles, who consecrated them through the laying on of hands so that their specific work could begin.

Once again, the precise title for the office held by these individuals (the Greek word *diakonous*) does not appear in Acts 6:1-6. What does appear in this passage are two references to the act of serving or "waiting on tables" that employ the verb forms *diakonia* and *diakonein*. The goal was not to create a position of authority but to meet an urgent need in the community by finding individuals who had the right spirit and qualifications to fulfill that role.

Acts 6:1-6 has long served as the passage that sets forth the essential role and responsibilities of those who would come to be known as deacons, and it hints at their appropriate relationship with those who would later occupy the position of pastor. We will explore these issues in more depth in chapter 2, as we look at the second biblical passage that has historically informed how black churches have understood the role of the deacon: 1 Timothy 3:8-13.

Notes

1. These books include Howard B. Foshee, *Now That You're a Deacon*, (Nashville: Broadman Press, 1975); Robert E. Naylor, *The Baptist Deacon*, (Nashville: Broadman Press, 1955); Harold Nichols, *The Work of the Deacon and the Deaconess*, (Valley Forge: Judson Press, 1964); T. Dewitt Smith, *The Deacon in the Black Baptist Church* (Church/Town Productions, 1983); and Henry Webb, *Deacons: Servant Models in the Church*, (Nashville: Broadman Press, 2001).

2. Ernst Haenchen, *The Acts of the Apostles* (Philadelphia: Westminster Press, 1971), 261–62.

3. C.S.C. Williams, *The Acts of the Apostles* (New York: Harper & Row, 1957), 96.
4. Howard Thurman, *With Head and Heart* (New York: Harcourt, Brace, and Jovanavich, 1979), 195.
5. Liston Pope, quoted in *White Protestantism and the Negro,* by David M. Reimers (New York: Oxford, 1965), 186.
6. Naylor, *The Baptist Deacon,* 7.
7. M. E. Hussey, "Deacon," in *The Dictionary of Christianity in America,* edited by Daniel G. Reid, et al. (Downers Grove, IL: InterVarsity Press, 1990), 344.
8. Hussey, 344.
9. In addition to these five familiar translations, I have drawn on scholarly translations provided by Johannes Munck, *The Acts of the Apostles,* The Anchor Bible Series (Garden City, NY: Doubleday, 1967), 55; and Ernst Haenchen, *The Acts of the Apostles,* 259.
10. J. Oswald Sanders, *Spiritual Leadership* (Chicago: Moody Press, 1967), 52.
11. A literal translation of Acts 6:3 was provided by Dr. Mitzi Smith, associate professor of New Testament at Ashland Theological Seminary with a PhD in New Testament Studies and Greek from Harvard University.
12. T. Dewitt Smith, *The Deacon in the Black Baptist Church,* 21.
13. Smith, *The Deacon in the Black Baptist Church,* 27.
14. Madeleine S. and J. Lane Miller, "Philip the Evangelist" in *The New Harper's Bible Dictionary* (New York: Harper & Row, 1973), 548; "Philip," in *The Interpreter's Dictionary of the Bible,* vol. 3 (Nashville: Abingdon Press, 1962), 785.

°Chapter 2°
The Office of the Deacon in 1 Timothy 3:8-13

As we have seen, Acts 6:1-7 offers a brief description of the qualities and characteristics desired among those to be brought before the twelve apostles when the office of the deacon was first conceived: "men of good reputation, full of the Holy Spirit and wisdom" (6:3). However, the majority of that passage focused on the work to be done rather than the qualities required of the people called upon to serve. In contrast, 1 Timothy 3:8-13 presents a much more complete listing of the characteristics expected of those who would serve as deacons.

By the time 1 Timothy was written (in the early AD 60s), the position of deacon seems to have been established as an ongoing office in the life of the church. While Acts 6 described the appointment of seven men to serve alongside the twelve apostles and minister to the daily needs of the first Christian community in Jerusalem, 1 Timothy addresses how various leadership positions should be filled in the churches that were by then scattered throughout Asia Minor and the wider Mediterranean region. We have also noted already that 1 Timothy 3:8-13 is the first passage in which the term *deacon* (*diakonoi*) is used to describe an actual office within the early church rather than the service that needs to be performed. Yet the focus of the passage is not so much the duties of the office as the personal qualities and the public lifestyle expected of those serving as deacons.

Preachers and Deacons Are Linked Again

Acts 6 indicates that seven men were appointed in the Jerusalem church to relieve the twelve apostles of the need to be concerned about the administration of the communal property. This allowed the twelve apostles to concentrate on the ministry of the word and prayer.

I appreciate the language of Robert Naylor who says, "Deacons can set preachers free not so much 'from' something as free to 'do something' that otherwise might remain undone."[1] First Timothy 3 similarly links the offices of preacher and deacon together. The discussion of the qualities of a deacon in verses 8-12 occurs right after the similar description of the qualities and characteristics of those who would be *episkopoi* (elder/bishop/pastor) in 1 Timothy 3:1-7.

Since 1 Timothy 3 offers no additional insight into the precise roles and responsibilities of those who serve as deacons, we may reasonably assume that the work of "waiting tables" and other service-oriented tasks continued to be the primary role of the deacon. Paul seemed to assume his readers were familiar with the work assigned to deacons, but wanted to make it clear what kind of people should be sought out for this consecrated position. While Acts 6:1-7 defined *what* a deacon did in the community of believers, 1 Timothy 3:8-13 defined *who* was qualified to serve as a deacon and *how* they were to conduct themselves.

There is some agreement among New Testament scholars that Paul laid out these qualities and characteristics for both elders and deacons because the people filling those positions, especially in the church in Ephesus, were far removed from the virtues Paul sets forth in this passage. Elders and deacons were behaving without morality or integrity. Paul's words in 1 Timothy were meant to correct that problem not only in Ephesus but also in other churches throughout Asia Minor.

How Should a Deacon Live?

In just a few verses, Paul lays out a number of qualifications and characteristics of a good deacon, and also defines the personal conduct expected of those who would serve in this role. He includes the following:

Reverent—Worthy of Respect—Dignified—Serious (3:8)

Deacons should be people whose character and demeanor cause others to look up to them and hold them in high regard. They should give evidence of emotional stability and personal integrity, and should be above reproach in the eyes of the community.

Nothing is worse for the church than when its deacons' conduct becomes the basis of gossip and rumors. Churches should avoid selecting deacons whose reputations have been sullied by the misdeeds mentioned in the verses that follow, including things like immorality, lying, drunkenness, and the pursuit of dishonest gain.

Sincere—Not Double-tongued (3:8)

This refers to telling the truth—and not altering or distorting the facts or changing one's story depending on the situation. The Greek word for *sincere* suggests a theatre performance where one actor played multiple roles simply by changing the wax mask he or she held in front of the face. To be sincere means to be "without wax"—having only one face or one role or one report to make.

Not Indulging in Much Wine—Not a Drunkard (3:8)

In societies throughout the Mediterranean region, wine was a standard, daily beverage. Unreliable sources of fresh drinking water made the use of wine as a beverage all the more common— which helps explain 1 Timothy 5:23, which says, "Stop drinking only water and use a wine because of your stomach and your frequent illnesses."

The issue for the deacon is not abstinence from all alcoholic beverages, but moderation so as to avoid becoming intoxicated. The abuse of alcohol—and today we might also include the abuse of other addictive substances—is unacceptable for anyone who serves as a deacon.

Not Greedy—Not Pursuing Dishonest Gain (3:8)

Deacons have had some role in handling the church's financial resources since Acts 6:1-7 when the twelve apostles placed the seven in charge of the distribution of the commonly held funds. Such a position requires persons who would never skim off a portion of the offering or benevolence funds for their own personal use. Similarly, since church members may seek the guidance of a respected deacon in the handling of their own finances, deacons should never use their trusted relationship with church members as an opportunity to "fleece the flock." Deacons should concentrate on what they can give to the church, not what they can gain from their service.

Holding the Deep Truths (Mystery) of the Faith with a Clear Conscience (3:9)

Belief in God is an act of faith, as is belief in the various doctrines of Christianity such as the incarnation, the resurrection, and atonement. Deacons should be persons who can embrace the faith without feeling embarrassed that they cannot always explain every aspect of what the Bible says or state definitively what God is doing or why God may have allowed something to happen.

There are times when all Christians might echo the words of the father in Mark 9:24: "Lord, I believe, help me overcome my unbelief." Professional theologians and biblical scholars still debate the meaning of certain aspects of the Christian faith. At times it is appropriate for a deacon to answer a hard question by saying with the prophet Ezekiel: "O sovereign LORD, you alone know" (37:3). Sometimes the best answer a deacon can offer to another church member's question is, "I don't know—but I will attempt to find out more and get back to you."

Having Been Tested (3:10)

Persons were not to be placed into the position of deacon without a trial period when their performance could be observed and evaluated. While no specific time period is given in this passage, it would presumably have been long enough for the prospective deacons to be tested in relationship to the qualities and characteristics in verses 8-9.

This is the basis for what is known as "walking deacons" or "trial deacons" in many Baptist churches. This is an interim period (usually one year) in which individuals perform all the duties of a deacon but have not yet been ordained or installed. Indeed, these people may not be established as deacons if they do not serve well and hold up under close scrutiny during this trial period (see chapter 4).

Nothing Being Found against Them (3:10)

This verse should not be read to suggest that some full-scale background check must go on during the trial period to see if any dirt or scandal can be uncovered. Hopefully, the personal character and backgrounds of prospective deacons were considered before they were ever approached initially about becoming a deacon. What is being said here is that if potential deacons have performed satisfactorily during their probationary period of testing or trial, they should then be allowed to continue in the position.

Likewise Their Wives—or Women Helpers Likewise (3:11)

Various translations suggest two different ways to understand this reference to women in verse 11. The first view contends that it is suggesting specific criteria for the wives of men who are appointed as deacons. In many ways those criteria mirror what's been said about deacons in the earlier verses—they are to be "worthy of respect, not malicious talkers, but temperate and trustworthy in everything" (3:11, TNIV). We'll say more about the wives of deacons in our discussion of verse 12.

The second view is that the women mentioned in this verse are not the wives of male deacons, but female helpers or women deacons who were also serving in the early church. Chapters 5 and 6 in this book will be devoted to the consideration of whether women should serve as deacons.

Husband of One Wife—Must Manage Children and Household Well (3:12)

The Greek words here might be best translated, "a man of one woman." Luke Timothy Johnson suggests that, in the context of the early Christian church, there are four things that could be intended by this criterion: "It could mean that the man was married once, and, if widowed, did not remarry. It could mean a man was monogamous and not polygamous in his married life. It could mean that a man was faithful to his wife without a mistress. It could mean that a man was married instead of celibate."[2]

In most Baptist churches the real question is whether this verse prohibits a man who has been divorced and then remarried from serving as a deacon. Divorce was practiced in the ancient world, but it was limited primarily to proven cases of immorality or marital infidelity. Matthew 19:3 is a reminder that some men in ancient Israel believed they could divorce their wives "for any and every reason," not solely on the grounds of adultery.[3] In responding to a question about divorce, Jesus clearly seems to disapprove of the practice, but he does recognize the Mosaic laws that governed its practice.

There is no clear prohibition against a divorced and remarried person becoming a deacon. However, a person whose marital infidelity led to divorce would probably have been excluded from the office of deacon based on the earlier requirement that deacons be persons "worthy of respect" (3:8). Persons who cannot remain faithful to their marital vows may not be able to remain faithful to their duties as a deacon.

The second phrase refers to the deacon's own household and family. This suggests that people who can manage the personalities and finances within their own homes may be able to transfer those skills to the management of those affairs of the church assigned to the deacon.

Those Who Have Served Well Gain an Excellent Standing (3:13)

Not everyone agrees that 1 Timothy 3:13 should be included with verses 8-12 as addressing the characteristics and qualifications for persons serving as deacons. What seems more likely is that verse 13 speaks to the benefits or blessings that come to those who serve faithfully as deacons. At the very least deacons will enjoy positions of honor and esteem within the faith community. Another possibility is that they might progress from deacon to another leadership position in the church—perhaps hinting that some deacons may move from the ministry of waiting on tables to the ministry of teaching and the word, as seems to have been the case with Stephen and Philip.[4]

Set Apart for Service

Our studies of 1 Timothy 3:8-13 and Acts 6:1-7 have made it clear that the office of the deacon in the church has a biblical foundation. In Acts 6, seven men were chosen by the community and consecrated by the apostles to serve the benevolence needs of the community. Those chosen were well known and highly regarded, possessing a spiritual maturity and a level of godly wisdom that would guide them. The seven were not called to join the ranks of the apostles nor to exercise oversight of the apostles' work. Instead, the seven were assigned the ministry of "waiting on tables" or serving the needs of the people—especially the neediest and most vulnerable—freeing the apostles to focus on their primary ministries of preaching and prayer.

We have just seen that 1 Timothy 3:8-13 offers additional detail about the qualities and characteristics necessary in deacons. They are to be well-respected persons of faith who speak honestly and truthfully. They are to avoid drunkenness and dishonest financial gain. They must possess humility in the face of the truth and mystery of the faith and should exhibit an exemplary lifestyle in their family relationships. If all these qualities line up, and if they are found faithful during a "test" period when their performance can be observed and evaluated, they may serve the church in this important role.

What must not be lost in this initial discussion of the biblical roots of the office of deacon is the fact that the roles and responsibilities discussed in both passages are concisely set forth in the Greek word for deacon, which is *diakonia*. Literally this word means "servant" or "helper." The office of the deacon was created so that someone chosen by the community and duly sanctioned and consecrated by the clergy could be entrusted with the urgent and ongoing work of serving the needs of the congregation.

This word *servant* should not suggest any parallel between the work of the deacon in the church and the servile status of an entire class of people in the Greco-Roman world of the first century. Deacons were not to be thought of as bond servants, indentured servants, household servants, or personal servants who worked for the elite in that society.

Roman society in ancient times allowed certain persons to maintain a wide array of servants who worked by obligation to meet the needs of their "owner" or "master." The critical difference between these servants and *diakonia* is that the former worked under legal obligation, having been purchased in the marketplace, captured in the context of warfare, or born into slavery or servitude. Unlike those servants of the secular world who served "at the will" of their masters or owners, deacons served voluntarily and with open hearts in support of the health and well being of the faith community.

The Bible Is Neither Static Nor Stagnant

I firmly believe that a careful and critical analysis of Acts 6:1-7 and 1 Timothy 3:8-13 is indispensable as the basis for understanding the role and responsibilities of the deacon. At the same time, it must be acknowledged that time has not stood still since the books of the Bible were written. There was no such thing as the Baptist church during the writing of the New Testament, much less the existence of the various black Baptist movements that have emerged primarily within the last 100 years.

As was pointed out in the previous chapter, historical and cultural forces unique to the experience of being black in America during the days of Jim Crow racism and legalized segregation played a major role in the shaping of the black church. Those same forces also helped to shape an understanding of the roles and responsibilities of both pastors and deacons within that particular religious community. Part of the peculiar ethos of the black religious experience was also the practice of itinerancy among black Baptist preachers. That has also greatly influenced and shaped the work of the deacon in the black Baptist church.

All this being said, it must be repeated that the office of deacon in the black Baptist church and beyond must not be viewed or perpetuated based upon the cultural currents of the last century of American life. Rather, as with every other aspect of the organization and operation of the Christian church in all of its varied forms and locations, there must be a diligent search for and a determined commitment to our authentic biblical roots. This is one of the great lessons from Martin Luther and the Protestant Reformation of which the Baptist church is an outgrowth.

Church practices can become commonplace even when they are not biblically based. Luther and his Reformation colleagues challenged the Roman Catholic Church of the sixteenth century to offer biblical support for commonly agreed upon doctrines and practices like papal infallibility, indulgences, and purgatory.

Luther's appeal to *sola scriptura* or "solely on the authority of scripture"[5] remains a reminder and a stern warning to all churches today, and especially to our Baptist churches which place so much emphasis on the Bible as the central authority for faith and practice. It is always important to stop and be sure the practices in which we engage are consistent with the teachings of Scripture to which we turn for authority, authenticity, and accountability.

While the church must be careful not to engage in practices that are not rooted in Scripture, it must be equally careful not to restrict the voice of Scripture into its first-century beginnings. Some aspects of the life of the early church recorded in the Bible have been held up as clear indicators of how church life should be managed for all time. There are some who argue that the contemporary American church must mimic the churches of ancient Israel in every way. Yet there may be some aspects of life in the first century that should not be directly transferred into the life of the church of the twenty-first century.

There is a principle in the study of the Bible known as *discontinuity*. This principle recognizes that there are aspects of life and faith that were in force during the biblical era that may no longer remain vital or important to our understanding of the faith today. For instance, early Christians were told by Paul that they could *discontinue* such practices as circumcision, the observance of feast days, the dietary restrictions of Leviticus, and the practice of animal sacrifice—all of which were in *continuous* practice prior to the life of Christ and the writings of Paul.

This observation about continuity and discontinuity in the Bible is especially relevant at this point in the present study, because it allows us to touch on changes in the status of women within the Judeo-Christian tradition between 1400 BC and AD 2010. How has the status of women changed in the intervening 3500 years, and what does that mean for the church of today? Does the fact that women were excluded from leadership roles in the patriarchal culture of ancient Palestine demand that they also be excluded from the roles of pastor or deacon in the church today?

It's clear that Acts 6:3 clearly expects that the seven people chosen to serve as the first deacons in the Jerusalem church would all be male—as were the twelve apostles. That being said, we have come to the point where we must ask whether the roles of preacher and deacon were meant to be reserved only for biological for all time, or if there would come a day when women could serve in these roles as well? We will turn to that important question in the fifth chapter of this book.

Notes

1. Robert E. Naylor, *The Baptist Deacon,* 9.
2. Luke Timothy Johnson, *The First and Second Letters to Timothy,* The Anchor Bible (Garden City, NY: Doubleday, 2001), 228.
3. Johnson, 213.
4. See chapter 1 of this book as well as Acts 7–8.
5. Roland Bainton, *Christendom,* vol. 2 (New York: Harper Torchbooks, 1964), 15, and *Here I Stand* (New York: Mentor Books, 1950), 288.

°Chapter 3°
Deacons in the Black Baptist Church

Having set forth the biblical passages that define the role and responsibilities of deacons (Acts 6:1-7) and that establish the characteristics desired of those chosen to serve as deacons (1 Timothy 3:8-13), the discussion now turns to the ways in which the work of the deacon has evolved from the first to the twenty-first century of the Christian church. This chapter gives special attention to the work of the deacon in the Baptist church in general, and in the black Baptist church in particular.

Henry Webb has pointed out that church history has seen something of a progression or evolution in the way the work of the deacon has been understood.[1] S. I. Stuber states that, in the first few centuries of the early Christian church, deacons were officials "whose responsibility was to care for the poor and needy in Christian communities."[2] Such an understanding is very much in keeping with the role assigned to the seven original deacons in Acts 6:1-7. Yet by the Middle Ages the role of the deacon had evolved primarily into that of a worship leader. Of course, this was before the emergence of the Protestant movement, at a time when serving as a deacon was a step on the way to being ordained as a priest in the Catholic Church. To this day, the Catholic Church maintains the office of deacon both in this historic form, and also a way by which married men can serve their local parishes as worship leaders, but without the authority to preside over the mass.[3]

Writing about the use of the term *deacon* in various Christian traditions, Harold Nichols notes:

> The Roman Catholic deacon is an assistant at the altar and is a member of the priesthood. The deacon in the Church of England is a member of the priesthood; he is given such ritualistic tasks as reading the gospel and assisting the priest, but he cannot consecrate the sacramental elements or pronounce absolution. The deacon in the congregational type of church is a layperson who is chosen by the church.[4]

Baptist churches and their deacons, of course, fall in the "congregational" category.

According to Webb, the Reformation of the sixteenth century brought with it several changes in the role of the deacon. In addition to establishing the fact that deacons were to be lay leaders and not members of the clergy, reformers such as Martin Luther and John Calvin rediscovered the biblical role of the deacon as a servant with an emphasis on delivering assistance and support to the poor and needy. But in the eighteenth and nineteenth centuries, we begin to see another shift among many Baptist and other Protestant churches. During this time, deacons and other lay leaders took on more of the administrative and supervisory work of the local church, with deacons often serving as a congregation's board of directors. Webb states:

> As a board of directors, deacons screened all major recommendations to determine whether they should go to the congregation. They controlled the finances, facilities, and other business affairs of the church. The pastor was directly responsible to the deacons rather than to the church.[5]

In his 1846 book, R. B. C. Howell referred to deacons as "the financial officers of the church" and as "the board of the church" or "the executive board of the church."[6] The classic J. Newton Brown work, *A Baptist Church Manual*, first published in 1853, seems to reinforce this understanding that the work of the deacon was not limited to spiritual matters, but also included some supervision of the temporal affairs of the church. Brown writes:

> It shall be the duty of the Deacons to seek out such members of the church as need pecuniary assistance, and to use the alms of the church for their relief; to visit the sick; to prepare and distribute the elements of the Lord's Supper; to take a general supervision of the temporal interests of the church, and to cooperate with and assist the pastor in the performance of his duties.[7]

A similar understanding is endorsed by Prince E. Burroughs, who in 1929 suggested a division of labor between clergy and deacons along spiritual and financial lines:

> On one side of the line stands the pastor. He is, shall we say, the ranking officer especially entrusted with the ministry which is more distinctly spiritual. On the other side is the deacon, standing next to the pastor and entrusted with the care of the material interests of the church. He is to care for the properties of the church, its buildings, its pastor's home, and its other material holdings. He is to direct and safeguard the financial side of its ministry.[8]

In this book's introduction, I observed that contemporary assumptions about the board of deacons as an administrative and supervisory body within the black Baptist church are likely being shaped by the growing class of African American professionals who bring their experiences of corporate America into the life of the congregation. While I believe this is true, these older sources we have cited suggest that the groundwork for this shift from servant to administrator, from a position of humility to a position of authority, began much earlier—and that the controversies surrounding that shift are long-standing.

Understanding the Shift

How did this shift in the role of the deacon come to pass? One might speculate that, as the early church grew and became increasingly more established and institutionalized, the practical matters concerning the community of faith became commensurately more complex. Whereas the first Christians met informally in one another's homes, later believers (more and more of whom were Gentiles) established central places of worship. Those buildings were surely encumbered with financial and material concerns—concerns related to rent or ownership, to cleaning and maintaining, to supplies of worship resources. The congregations themselves were growing, and so the shared financial and materials resources were greater—but so, certainly, were the people's needs.

We have already observed that growth and change in the church brings new challenges and stress. The office of deacon was established in the time of growth immediately after the first Pentecost to relieve the apostles of pragmatic responsibilities that took away from their time and energies and devotion to prayer and teaching the gospel. It must have seemed logical as the generations passed to delegate other, similarly practical responsibilities to the deacons.

Henry Webb is among those who lament this shift in the understanding of the work of the deacon. He states, "This view of the deacons as church business managers tended to distract from the other areas of service previously given strong attention."[9] Webb's observation points to a fundamental question that confronts every pastor, every deacon, and every Baptist congregation be it black or white or Asian or Hispanic: Is the deacon primarily a servant leader in the church, or should the deacon also exercise leadership in the oversight and operation of the day-to-day financial and operational affairs of the congregation?

Many classic studies of the work of the deacon have attempted to address this question. Some support the corporate board approach or the so-called "boss mentality" that seems to be so prevalent in many churches today. Others push the emphasis in the opposite direction, moving away from deacons playing an oversight and administrative role over the financial affairs of the church and toward deacons as those who work with the pastor in providing service to the church.

One of the most notable books moving the understanding of the deacon's work in the direction of a serving role is *Now That You're a Deacon* by Howard Foshee. He begins his discussion by expressing regret that the term "board of deacons" was ever coined. The idea of deacons as a board of directors is, according to Foshee, "foreign to how Baptists should work together."[10] He quotes a Baptist deacon who spoke at an ordination service for other deacons who offered a very different understanding of the role of the deacon:

> A person is not made a deacon just for the honor, although it is an honor beyond most of the things that can come to a man's life. The deacon is set apart to serve; he is committed to serve God and his fellow man. As a new deacon, you must understand that you have not been elected to an "official board" to exercise authority in the life of the church. The office of deacon is not an office of authority but one of service.[11]

One of the standard guidelines for maintaining order in the Baptist church is *The Hiscox Guide for Baptist Churches*. This study, originally published in 1859 and updated as recently as 1975, seems to point away from any understanding of the deacon exercising any authority over the temporal affairs of the church. Hiscox writes:

> The secular concerns of the church, including its financial affairs, would seem legitimately to be embraced in the duties of the deaconship according to the original purpose, as belonging to its temporalities, but now these matters are usually committed to an entirely different class of men known as trustee, elected under the specific direction of State laws.[12]

Hiscox offers a clear rationale for a shift back to a biblical model for the office of deacon as primarily a ministry of service and benevolence, delegating the fiscal, property, and personnel matters of the church to a newer ministry, the board of trustees. He provides further argument for the differentiated ministry of deacon and trustee by emphasizing the responsibilities that should draw the primary focus of deacons:

> Deacons should be watchful guardians of the purity and good order of the churches, striving to maintain a healthful tone of Christian faith and activity in the body. But they must act only in conjunction with the pastor, not independent of him, except possibly in very rare and urgent cases. Hence, while it is desirable for the pastor to have meetings with his deacons often or statedly for consultation and advice, it is not proper for them to hold meetings as a board of deacons, independent of and without the advice of the pastor.[13]

Although the present muddle concerning the role and responsibilities of deacons in the Baptist church is not a recent issue, we can now understand the origins of the confusion and some of the complexities behind the evolution of the role. A church that clearly establishes the mission and purview of the board of trustees as distinct and separate from the board of deacons will find itself better equipped and positioned to meet all the needs of the congregation—for spiritual teaching, prayer, visitation, benevolence, stewardship of material resources, and maintenance and administration related to the church's physical building and assets.

Clarifying the Responsibilities of All Ministries

It is impossible to evaluate or reconsider the role of the deacon in the Baptist church without considering the larger picture of the church and its ministries. Before any congregation launches into a full-scale analysis or rethinking of the office of the deacon, I would recommend its engaging in a process of considering all the ministries at work in their congregation. How would it empower and equip your leaders and laity if they had clear, well-articulated understandings of the mission and responsibilities of any given ministry? Imagine the increase in congregational involvement if all members understood exactly what they are committing to do by joining this ministry versus that one. Envision the improved relationships between church leaders and ministry heads if everyone grasped the specific call and tackled the particular needs their group has been tasked with addressing.

In most of our churches, the lines have become blurred and the roles have developed inefficient overlap in responsibilities. Clear communication makes corrective action creative and constructive. Before we go any further in considering the particulars of the deacon's role, let's take a quick look at some of the other key roles in a functioning Baptist church:

The Pastor

Having served as a pastor myself for more than thirty-five years, I am well aware of the many abuses of that office of which my colleagues and I may be guilty. I have seen pastors who view their congregations as human ATMs, designed to provide the pastor with money on demand. I am aware of pastors involved in sex scandals of every kind—adult and child, married and unmarried, heterosexual and homosexual, substantiated and also unsubstantiated. I recognize the practice of favoritism over competence when it comes to filling leadership positions in the church. I have seen pastors exploit members by using them as unpaid personal assistants to carry pulpit robes and Bibles, pick up personal dry cleaning, wash a personal vehicle, and run personal errands.

Pastors should clearly understand their role through the lens of Acts 20:28, which calls us to keep watch over the flock of which the Holy Spirit has made us overseers. Pastors too quickly embrace the word *overseers* for themselves, neglecting to notice that Paul also challenges leaders to keep watch first over *ourselves*. He urges such watchfulness, over self and the people, because he fears "savage wolves will come in among you, not sparing the flock" (Acts 20:29). Paul makes his warning even more forceful and relevant to this book when he adds: "Some even from your own group will come distorting the truth in order to entice the disciples to follow them" (Acts 20:30). When I watch religious broadcasting, I sometimes hear preachers who seem to fulfill Paul's prophecy in verse 30; many television preachers (and they are not the only offenders) are far more interested in fleecing the flock of God than they are in feeding them.

Jesus' words to the twelve apostles offer a central principle around which all pastors and spiritual leaders might be centered:

> You know that the rulers of the Gentiles lord it over them, and their great ones are tyrants over them. It will not be so among you; but whoever wishes to be great among you must be your servant, and whoever wishes to be first among you must be your slave; just as the Son of Man came not to be served but to serve, and to give his life as a ransom for many. (Matthew 20:25-28)

Another good description of the work of the pastor can be found in Jeremiah 3:15, which says, "I will give you shepherds [pastors, KJV] after my own heart who will feed you with knowledge and understanding."

Pastors are the primary caregivers to the flock of God, with a ministry extending to every area of the life of the congregation. The pastor does most of the preaching and teaching, presides over the visioning and business dimensions of the life of the church, and provides a context within which members of the church pursue personal spiritual formation. However, as reflected in the story in Acts 6:1-7, some assignments pastors can and should delegate to other reliable individuals in the congregation.

The Ushers

Many ushers point with pride to the words of Psalm 84:10: "I would rather be a doorkeeper in the house of my God than live in the tents of wickedness." Indeed, the work of the usher seems simple enough: Greet people at the doors of the church, provide them with worship bulletins if needed, and answer any questions about the location of the nursery, the restrooms, or a water fountain. All that being done, the usher escorts people to available seats and then returns to the door to serve other worshippers as they enter. Other tasks are assigned to the ushers based upon the particular structure of any autonomous Baptist congregation.

Simple and straightforward? Yes. Insignificant? Absolutely not! This task of welcoming strangers and members alike to the sanctuary of our God is of vital importance. First impressions, after all, are critical! It is heartbreaking when a doorkeeper in the house of the Lord fosters a spirit of wickedness, arrogance, or impatience. Therefore, ushers should be at their posts on time, be well informed about the physical facility and the available ministries, and offer worshipers a warm welcome, a pleasant smile, and the humble service of a timely answer or a gracious escort.[14]

Music Ministry

Music plays a leading role in most black Baptist worship services, and the singers and musicians who provide that music occupy an honored place in the life of the congregation. W. E. B. Du Bois observed that "the preacher, the music, and the frenzy constitute an essential core to the black church experience."[15] The style and form of the music may vary from one black church to another, including hymns that range from nineteenth-century Negro spirituals to European anthems, and gospel sounds stretching from Charles Albert Tindley and Thomas A. Dorsey to the contemporary sounds of Kirk Franklin and Yolanda Adams. Virtually any style is appropriate, as long as the music glorifies God.

There should be no room in any church's music ministry for temperamental musicians, egotistical performers, or power-hungry directors. Each element of the worship service should point the people toward God, not to any human being, no matter how talented the vocalist, how accomplished the organist— or how charismatic the preacher! The music ministry should be committed to worship and the Word—and to bringing the Word through music and the blending of all the gifts God has entrusted to that ministry.

Trustees

Unlike most other positions in the church today, the office of the trustee is one that has no real biblical precedent. The pastor has the apostles as role models; the music ministry has Miriam and the Levites; the ushers and greeters have the temple doorkeepers; the deacons have Stephen and Phoebe (see chapter 5), among others. The trustee, however, emerged as a pragmatic adaptation of a secular role. As the churches and denominations grew, and as the state became aware of the vast resources entrusted to the church—resources of land, cash, and other capital assets, the government began to require financial accountability. Someone in the church had to assume fiduciary responsibility for the administration of church finances and business affairs.

If the apostles recognized the drain of administrating benevolence among the hundreds in their care, how much more do churches today acknowledge the complex and high-stakes demands of overseeing the property, finances, and other legal matters affecting churches in the twenty-first century? The church clearly needs someone to manage these affairs of church and state, and thus was born the board of trustees. While good stewardship clearly has extensive roots in Scripture, the trustee ministry employs extensive knowledge and experience gained in corporate America and the business world. For that reason, common wisdom and practice recommends the election of trustees from among church members who work in for-profit and not-for-profit organizations. However, since the board of trustees uses the corporate model of a board of directors, it is not surprising that tension arises when pragmatic financial concerns conflict with ministry concerns.

I have heard the phrase "tricky trustees" about as many times as I have heard the phrase "devilish deacons." Perfectly wonderful people, when elected as trustees in the Baptist church, can be possessed by a strange and sudden sense of ownership. Regrettably, the word *fiduciary* suddenly seems more important than the word *faithful*. An effective pastor and a Spirit-led chair of the trustees should work as partners to establish a godly and respectful goal of faithful fiduciary management. Collecting, counting, banking, and wisely investing the church's money are invaluable to today's church, especially in an economy where endowments (if they exist) are hard hit and the future stability of the church is at risk. Trustees have the responsibility of securing the future through wise stewardship of the church's financial resources.

The Congregation

No survey of the major roles in the black Baptist church could be considered completely without a focus on the role of the congregation. The Baptist church lives and breathes on the principle of congregational autonomy and congregational authority. That means every Baptist church is free to run itself without any interference from outside its ranks—and that the ministry is funded and facilitated by its members. The people do the work of the trustees, deacons, ushers, Christian educators, counselors, etc., and they sustain that work through their own giving—not through a denominational budget or subsidy. It is an exciting and empowering model for being the church and doing the work of the Lord.

The problem arises from the so-called 80/20 principle. Most Baptist churches I know run on this principle, which observes that 80 percent of the membership supplies just 20 percent of the money and ministry service needed for a church to fulfill its mission goals from year to year. Conversely, 20 percent of the membership provides 80 percent of the annual revenue and 80 percent of the time and effort needed for the church to operate.

Far too many of our congregations are comprised of people who come to church only when the senior pastor is preaching, only when their favorite choir is singing, or only when their ministry group is actively involved. Some members of my congregation in Cleveland have told me in no uncertain terms that they will be absent on any Sunday when a meeting of their sorority or a Cleveland Browns home football game is scheduled! And even among those who would never miss Sunday worship, there are many who seem to love the Lord with all their heart, mind, soul, and strength only for those two hours each week, after which they do not want to be involved—not in outreach or prayer meetings, not in Bible studies or children's ministry. A church cannot be effective and faithful to the work of Jesus Christ if the vast majority of its members are committed to worship without a corresponding commitment to working for Christ in the church, the community, and the wider world.

My point in this section is not to offer an exacting description of every important ministry or church committee. The role of other ministries is covered extensively in other books, including the highly specific and practical "Work of the Church" series published by Judson Press. Yet as we continue to consider the specific role of the deacon in the black Baptist church, we must always remember that the deacon does not function in a vacuum. Christian ministry is most effective and empowered when all members participate and when all participants clearly understand their call, roles, and responsibilities. This is true not only of deacons or those in the other ministries I've highlighted, but also of every ministry, board, committee, and individual in the church.

Cultural Depictions of Deacons

T. Dewitt Smith's *The Deacon in the Black Baptist Church* was the first scholarly study done on the precise topic of the role of deacons in the black church tradition. But when it comes to how people understand the role of the deacon, several popular depictions have been quite influential. Unfortunately, these nonbiblical characterizations have contributed to a further distortion of how this position is understood.

Perhaps the most influential recent depiction came from a popular situational comedy called *Amen,* which ran on NBC from 1986 to 1991 and continues to appear in syndication. The show featured African American comedian Sherman Hemsley as Deacon Ernest Frye, alias "The Deacon." Deacon Frye was an attorney in Philadelphia, Pennsylvania, and he brought that sense of authority and prominence with him into his church position. His reserved parking space at the church was marked by a sign declaring, "Don't even think about parking here." The swagger with which he walked through the church left no doubt in any viewer's mind that this man not only "ran the church" but also ran the pastor.

Nothing about Hemsley's caricature of the black Baptist deacon remotely suggests a servant leader who plays a supportive role in the church. Instead, this widely viewed TV series depicted the deacon as a powerful figure who sought to rule over the church. Clearly, that depiction is far removed from the understanding of the role and responsibilities of the deacon as established by Acts 6. But, like the distorted images of the black preacher found in films, TV shows, and literature, this depiction of the deacon in a black church has been viewed in homes across the United States for many years, and continues to influence how the role is understood.

We find equally troubling depictions of the black deacon throughout black literature. In *The Oxford Companion to African American Literature,* the entry on "Preachers and Deacons"

written by Elon Kuli says nothing about either role in terms of
servant leadership or work done on behalf of the congregation.
Instead, the offices of preacher and deacon are linked together as
the butt of jokes and scorn within African American folk literature and culture. For example, Kuli writes:

> The preacher and his deacon (if the two did not have an
> adversarial role grounded in competition) were also pictured
> in jokes as being greedy materialists who always wanted
> more money, bigger cars, and more expensive suits . . .
> Another mark of the preacher/deacon is his unending sexual
> pursuit of the good sisters inside and outside church.[16]

Given the important role played by the deacon in the black
Baptist church, and the trouble that can erupt in the church
due to misunderstandings about the roles and responsibilities
of that office, we must challenge such distorted images of what
it means to be a deacon. Yet even as we focus on a more biblical
understanding of the office of the deacon, it's also important to
remember that these nonbiblical depictions are likely based on
their creators' experiences with real deacons and that such depictions (and experiences) continue to influence how deacons
in the black Baptist church are perceived.

Pastors and Deacons

Perhaps more than any other concern related to the office of the
deacon, it is the relationship between the black Baptist pastor
and the board of deacons that generates the most tension and
controversy. Baptist churches in the United States have been
debating and dividing over this relationship for at least two
hundred years, and nowhere is that debate and division more
prevalent than in our black churches. At the heart of the debate
is a single question: Is the deacon's job to oversee and regulate
the ministry of the pastor, or is the deacon's job to serve the
needs of the people in support of the pastor?

Any consideration of this relationship between pastor and deacon must take into account the unique history and cultural distinctives of the black Baptist church. Needless to say, some significant historical and cultural differences separate the operation of black Baptist churches from their white Baptist counterparts. Perhaps the most important of those differences involves the heightened influence and importance black clergy have enjoyed in their communities from the slave era to the present. While authority in some white Baptist churches has gradually drifted toward lay leadership, such a transfer of power and authority from the clergy to the laity never completely occurred in most black churches. Without understanding the unique role of the preacher throughout African American history, it is impossible to understand how misunderstandings over the role of deacon in the black Baptist church have led to tensions, church schisms, pastoral dismissals, wholesale dismissal of groups of deacons, and other conflicts.[17]

This historic tension between deacon as servant leader and deacon as boss of both church and pastor is very much alive and at work in black Baptist churches. In *Church Administration in the Black Perspective,* Floyd Massey and Samuel McKinney capture this tension quite well:

> Some deacons consider themselves the church's spiritual fathers, ruling elders who serve and assist the pastor in the shepherding of the flock, and, as a rule, have been basically loyal to the pastor and the church, in spite of pressure brought on them to function differently. . . . On the other hand, there have been deacons and other officers who felt it their solemn and sworn duty to *protect* the congregation *from* the pastor. Others considered themselves as employers and subsequently the "boss" of the pastor. (emphasis added)[18]

C. Eric Lincoln and Lawrence H. Mamiya hint at certain factors that might contribute to the dual role of the deacon involving both spiritual and secular concerns. They observe:

The duties of the deacon may vary from church to church
. . . but in general they are to assist the pastor in maintaining
the quality of the spiritual life of the church. They assist
with communion, visit the sick, care for the needy, conduct
devotional services, and administer the affairs of the church
in the absence of a pastor.[19]

That final phrase—"in the absence of a pastor"—may offer
significant insight into how the role of the deacon as "boss"
took root in the black Baptist church.

Church Leadership "in the Absence of a Pastor"

The practice of itinerant clergy was commonplace in black
Baptist churches for many years. Most people associate the
word *itinerancy* with the Methodist Church around the time of
the Great Awakening from 1735–1750. It calls to mind preachers who traveled from town to town and church to church
without having any single permanent preaching location. One
can imagine men like John Wesley, George Whitfield, Gilbert
Tennent, and others preaching hundreds of sermons every
year in dozens of different locations. The term itinerancy later
evolved into the Methodist practice of clergy being moved by
a bishop from one church assignment to another every three to
five years.[20]

There is, however, another understanding of itinerancy that
has long been practiced by black Baptists. This involves one
pastor serving multiple congregations at the same time. A pastor might preach for a certain church or group of churches on
the first and third Sundays of the month and a different church
or group of churches on the second and fourth Sundays. A pastor serving multiple congregations might even visit each church
only once a month. T. Dewitt Smith recognizes this practice
when he writes, "The pastor, having more than one congregation, was really no more than the 'special preacher' for the
Sunday that particular church met for worship."[21]

So what happened in the worship service on the other three Sundays? Who handled the operation and oversight of the church during weeks when there was no pastoral presence? Who administered, oversaw, and managed church affairs when the pastor was only present for portions of one or two days each month? As Smith further notes, "In most places, any and all business transacted through the week and during the month was taken care of by the deacon board, especially the chairman."[22] It is all too easy to understand how deacons who have operated in churches where the pastor was an itinerant might expect to hold similar occupational or pastoral authority even when a full-time pastor is present.

Consider as well the number of black people who migrated from the South to the North and West during the Great Migration between 1895 and 1945. Many of them came from rural settings where itinerancy was the practice and church power and authority was in the hands of the deacons. That mindset may well have remained with them when they joined churches in their new hometowns.

Itinerancy, while still present in some places, is no longer as common as it once was in the black Baptist church. Today, most black Baptist churches are led by a full-time or part-time pastor who serves only that congregation. Nevertheless, it is very likely that the practice of itinerancy, which shaped black church life for decades, helped create a model of church governance that has greatly contributed to existing tensions between pastors and deacons.

Who Governs When the Pulpit Is Vacant?

Churches are also forced to operate "in the absence of a pastor" in times of pastoral transition, when one pastor has left and a new pastor has yet to be called. In some cases that time of transition can stretch on for two or more years. If the current pastor dies suddenly or decides to retire or resign unexpectedly, the result is the same: the church now finds itself in the absence of a pastor. In these times the church may look to its deacons for guidance, direction, and a sense of continuity.

In some churches there may be provisions in the constitution or by-laws for such situations. It may be clearly spelled out that "in the absence of a pastor" the authority and responsibilities associated with that office are transferred temporarily to another person or group. Perhaps an interim pastor will be called. Perhaps other ministers already in the church will take on more responsibility. Perhaps the former pastor's spouse, children, or siblings will assume leadership of that congregation. Or it may fall to the deacons to carry on until a new pastor has been called and installed.

Two things should be pointed out at this point. First, any church that does not have a stated policy on what should happen when the pulpit is vacant is asking for trouble, because that eventuality may occur without much warning. Second, every church needs to understand that those who exercised leadership "in the absence of a pastor" may not be eager to yield their power and influence simply because a new pastor has been called. Deacons and others who lead the church through a transition time may grow attached to their newfound influence and may be reluctant to let go. Here, too, a clear policy is helpful if not essential.

What Happens When the Pastor Is Incapacitated?

Similar dynamics may be present when a pastor faces a prolonged sickness or is otherwise incapacitated and unable to fulfill the duties of the office. Most churches do not worry if the pastor is away for a few weeks; they experience such short-term vacancies with annual vacation schedules. What is more difficult is when a few weeks stretches into a few months or more. Who governs the church and oversees its operations if the pastor faces long-term incapacitation?

I have known churches where medical situations kept the pastor away for as long as six months. These times create a leadership vacuum, and persons come from every direction to fill that leadership role. Very often it is the deacons who are charged with overseeing the operations of the church until the pastor returns. They are expected to identify persons who will preach each week, and to handle any weddings, funerals, baby christenings, and other pastoral tasks that are called for "in the absence of a pastor."

This is a challenging time for everyone. Technically, the church still has a pastor, yet the work assigned to the pastor goes undone unless someone steps in. I have known of instances when deacons served as the leadership group while the pastor was incapacitated and eventually made a clean transition back to the pastor's leadership. But I have also known of instances when some deacons did not rejoice over the pastor's return to good health because they had grown accustomed to exercising the power and influence of the pastoral office.

Moving from Historical Consequences Back to Original Intent

Throughout the history of the black Baptist church, circumstances have often arisen that have forced deacons to fill a leadership position. Our churches have found themselves operating in the absence of a pastor due to itinerancy, the cultural impact of the Great Migration, sudden vacancies in the pastoral position, or the long-term incapacitation of a pastor. Our churches have often coped with these situations by looking to deacons for leadership, sometimes to the point of claiming that the deacon's most appropriate role is to oversee the work of the pastor.

Such a journey through the history and tradition of how the role of deacon has evolved in the black Baptist church is important and informative. Yet the question that remains is whether our churches today are operating with an understanding of the work of the deacon that is informed primarily by Scripture rather than by recent history and tradition. With this question in mind, let us now return our attention to the careful and deliberate training of deacons so that churches can prepare and equip persons to serve in a way that is consistent with the biblical model of *diakonos* or servant leadership.

Notes

1. Henry Webb, *Deacons: Servant Models in the Church* (Nashville: Broadman and Holman, 2001), 64–65.
2. S. I. Stuber, "Deacon" in *The Illustrated Bible and Church Handbook* (New York: Association Press, 1966), 91.
3. M. E. Hussey, "Deacon," in *The Dictionary of Christianity in America*, 344.
4. Nichols, *The Work of the Deacon and the Deaconess*, 10.
5. Webb, 65.
6. R. B. C. Howell, *The Deaconship* (Philadelphia: American Baptist Publication Society, 1846), 12.
7. J. Newton Brown, *A Baptist Church Manual* (Valley Forge, PA: Judson Press, 1983), 28.
8. P. E. Burroughs, *Honoring the Deaconship* (Nashville: The Southern Baptist Convention Press, 1929), 17.
9. Webb, 65.
10. Howard B. Foshee, *Now That You're a Deacon*, 13.
11. Foshee, 14.
12. Edward T. Hiscox, *The Hiscox Guide for Baptist Churches* (Valley Forge, PA: Judson Press, 1975), 74.
13. Hiscox, 74.
14. For more on the specific role of the usher, see Alvin D. Johnson, *The Work of the Usher* (Valley Forge, PA: Judson Press, 1966).
15. W. E. B. Du Bois, "Of the Faith of the Fathers" in *The Souls of Black Folk* (Boston: Bedford Books, 1997), 149.
16. Elon Kuli, "Preachers and Deacons" in *The Oxford Companion to African American Literature* (New York: Oxford, 1997), 598.
17. In his landmark study, *The Deacon in the Black Baptist Church*, T. Dewitt Smith considers how these matters are uniquely and distinctly associated with the history and experiences of the black Baptist church.

18. Floyd Massey Jr. and Samuel Berry McKinney, *Church Administration in the Black Perspective* (Valley Forge, PA: Judson Press, 2003), 31. Emphasis added.
19. C. Eric Lincoln and Lawrence H. Mamiya, *The Black Church in the African American Experience* (Durham, NC: Duke University Press, 1990), 42–43.
20. Daniel Reid and Robert Linder, *The Dictionary of Christianity in America*, 583.
21. T. Dewitt Smith, *The Deacon in the Black Baptist Church*, 77.
22. Ibid.

Chapter 4

Training for Deacons in Today's Black Church

The seven individuals named in Acts 6:1-7 were selected by the Jerusalem church and immediately consecrated and set to work by the apostles. In contrast, in the black Baptist church of the twenty-first century, it is considered desirable that persons chosen to be deacons should go through a carefully designed period of training before they begin their term of service. That training period typically lasts for one year, and during that time the candidates for the position of deacons are known as trial deacons or walking deacons.

This twelve-month time frame is a probationary period during which two important things occur. First, the church observes the candidates to see how seriously they are taking their new duties. For example, are the trial deacons regular in their church attendance, and are they faithful in carrying out any and all duties assigned to them during this time? Second, the trial deacons can determine whether or not serving as a deacon for a full term, which in the black Baptist church is often a life term, is something they really want to do. Those trial deacons who complete the training period are then accepted for ordination or whatever installation service the local church deems appropriate.

What will be presented in this chapter is not a set curriculum that every church should follow. What I have learned in my nearly forty years in the ministry is that few if any black Baptist churches are going to adopt an entire training program designed for use by all congregations! What tends to happen is that pastors and churches pick and choose from among many available resources the kind of curriculum that best suits their taste and serves their interests. Recognizing that reality, what is offered in this chapter is an outline of topics and issues that should be considered in creating a training program intended to prepare incoming deacons.

The issues raised in this chapter are not drawn out of thin air. Instead, they are the questions and concerns I have personally seen churches and deacons struggle with over the last forty years of my own ministry in the black Baptist church. I began as an assistant to the pastor at Bethany Baptist Church of Brooklyn, New York, in 1971. I served as associate pastor at Abyssinian Baptist Church of New York City from 1972–76. I served as pastor of St. Paul Baptist Church in Montclair, New Jersey, from 1976–86. I have been pastor of Antioch Baptist Church of Cleveland, Ohio, since 1987.

Not wanting to rely solely on my own experience, however, I consulted with more than forty other pastors and congregations as part of this project. Our collective experiences have guided and shaped the issues raised in this chapter. The results are some invaluable hints and suggestions for pastors and deacon boards to consider for themselves. Each church will need to evaluate not only which suggestions they might implement, but also how and by whom the training material will be presented. I recommend a committee approach to conducting such training. In such a model, a group of current deacons may both mentor and motivate trial deacons through the process.

Most churches will prefer to draft or compile a training curriculum that has been mutually agreed upon by both the pastor and current board of deacons.

Baptist Distinctives

The training curriculum should cover every aspect of the work of the deacon, beginning with a clear understanding of Baptist distinctives including, but not limited to, local church autonomy, the principle of regional and national association, the meaning of the ordinances of the Lord's Supper and believers' baptism by immersion, the authority of Scripture, and the separation of church and state.[1]

Beyond addressing those Baptist distinctives that are universal to Baptist churches around the world, deacon training should give careful attention to the unique practices of the local Baptist church that has selected these candidates to serve as their deacons. Such training might encompass the by-laws or constitution used to govern the corporate life of the congregation. Trial deacons might also be provided with an organizational flow chart both for the day-to-day operation of the church as well as for the process by which policy decisions are made. Who presides at congregational meetings? What constitutes a quorum at such meetings? What, if any, is the role of the deacons in the policy-making process of the church? Where does responsibility for the financial life of the congregation rest? What, if any, is the deacons' role in fiduciary matters?

The training should remind trial deacons that, given the reality of local church autonomy, the roles and responsibilities of the deacon often vary from one congregation to another. What a deacon does in one Baptist church may have no bearing whatsoever on what deacons may be called on to do in another Baptist congregation. In fact, when persons who have served as deacons in one Baptist congregation transfer membership to another church, generally speaking they do not also transfer that title or position with them. This differs from the ordination of clergy, which brings a status recognized by state and federal law. As such, clergy are recognized beyond the confines of a local congregation and their credentials may generally be transferred to or recognized by another church or denomination. In contrast, the ordination of deacons is an action limited to the life of a local church. (See ordination section on p. 73.)

Baptist Churches and the Associational Principle

While Baptist churches are self-governed bodies that operate under the principle of local church autonomy, it would be wise to remind trial deacons of the equally important Baptist distinctive of association. The associational principle reminds Baptist churches that while our internal congregational life is determined without any interference or involvement from some external authority, the work and witness of the local church can be greatly enhanced if and when we agree to partner with other like-minded Baptist congregations. Some things, such as global missions, scholarship support for colleges and seminaries, and public witness on issues of social justice, local churches cannot address adequately alone. However, when several Baptist churches collaborate through the associational principle, together we can have a greater impact in those areas.

During their training period, introduce trial deacons to the groups and alliances with which your local church is in association. This would include all local, regional, and national bodies, including ministerial alliances, state and national conventions, and global groups such as the Baptist World Alliance. Affiliation with these organizations may be reflected in the church budget, on the annual church calendar, and in the active involvement of the pastor and other members of the church. It is helpful to pastor, parishioners, and community members alike when deacons can speak intelligently and convincingly about the local church's involvement in ministries and matters beyond their own congregation.

Deacons and the Worship Life of the Church

Most Baptist churches have some expectation of how deacons should participate in the worship services of the church. In some churches deacons are expected to lead or share in a devotional period of 10–15 minutes before the regularly scheduled worship service begins. This might include reading Scripture and leading in prayer and congregational singing.

Usually deacons' leadership in worship is not limited to Sunday morning services. The same is often expected during seasonal revivals, midweek services, and occasional Sunday afternoon programs that still occur in many black Baptist churches. This would extend to those occasions when more than one congregation worships together, whether to mark a liturgical holiday, to honor a board or ministry of the church, or to celebrate a church or pastoral anniversary. New deacons should clearly understand what is expected of them in such settings, both as individuals or as a group.

Deacons and the Bible

Since deacons serve in a biblically based office and since Baptist deacons are expected to place primary emphasis on the authority of Scripture, I highly recommend making a thorough study of Acts 6:1-7 and 1 Timothy 3:8-13 part of your training. Thus, trial deacons will gain understanding of the biblical foundations for their position. This also allows you to introduce the position as one that centers on service offered and not authority assumed.

Most churches will agree that deacons should be encouraged to develop a general familiarity with the content and composition of the Bible beyond those foundational texts. First Timothy 3:9 may say that deacons should hold the mystery of the faith with a clear conscience, but the Bible itself should not be entirely a mystery to deacons! As spiritual leaders of the congregation, deacons should be able to find their way among the 66 books of the Bible without having to turn to the index page. Deacons often find themselves at the bedside or graveside of a member of the congregation, and it is not unusual for parishioners or family members to ask for a specific passage of Scripture. What a wonderful witness it would be if every deacon has been trained in such a way that she or he could turn to that passage without having to fumble through the pages! This level of familiarity may take some time, but I recommend some basic biblical education as part of your deacon training.

At the same time, some parts of the Bible remain legitimate mysteries even for the most seasoned biblical scholar. Passages concerning God's judgment, miracles, the virgin birth, Christ's work of atonement, the end times, and second coming of Jesus are shrouded in a mystery that is not easily penetrated. If and when a deacon is approached by a church member or anyone else with a Bible question, the true meaning of 1 Timothy 3:9 should always prevail. They should hold the mystery of the faith with a clear conscience. This means, in part, that a deacon should never be afraid to acknowledge to a church member what they do not know, especially if the question or text is not easily knowable.

A great humility attends the words "I do not know." When a question demands such a humble answer, deacons might be advised to bring such questions and concerns to the pastor for clarification. Trial deacons should be encouraged to seek help from their deacon mentor, and of course deacons old and new may do some guided research and take the findings back to those who raised the question. Whatever strategy or protocol your church recommends to its deacons, be sure to establish that no deacon is expected to possess the answer to every question about the Bible. Better to say "I don't know" than to attempt a brash or false reply without understanding.

Deacons and the Ordinances

Baptist churches speak of ordinances while many other Christian denominations speak of sacraments. Baptists observe two ordinances while other Christian groups observe as many as seven. Here is another area where trial deacons should be instructed so they can fully understand and be able to explain these Baptist distinctives.

A sacrament is "a religious ceremony in which a certain visible act, accompanied by faith, is believed to impart the blessing of God upon the one who shares in it."[2] Some Christian groups refer to the sacraments as "an outward and visible sign of an inward and spiritual grace given unto us ordained by Christ himself."[3] The Roman Catholic Church lists seven sacraments: Baptism (of infants as well as new adult converts), penance, holy Eucharist (the Lord's Supper), confirmation (of baptismal vows), holy orders (ordination to the ministry), matrimony, and anointing of the sick (with oil). In each of these instances, sacramental theology asserts, a person who shares in the sacrament receives through it an actual impartation of grace that effects an inward transformation in the participant.

The Baptist church holds a different view on these matters, and it is crucial that deacons be familiar with these differences so they can help others understand why their local church worships as it does. First of all, Baptists observe only two acts that are "enjoined by Christ for perpetual observance in his church."[4] Those two acts are baptism and the Lord's Supper. Baptists find nowhere in Scripture that Christ establishes for all believers any of the other practices considered sacred by the Catholic Church. Moreover, most Baptists avoid use of the word *sacrament*, preferring the term *ordinance*, which derives from the idea that the act has been ordered or ordained by Jesus, with the expectation that his followers throughout time will observe that act. Unlike a sacrament, which assumes the act brings about the inward change for which it is the outward sign, an ordinance is considered an outward sign of an inward change that has already transpired.

Baptism. In training new deacons about the ordinance of baptism, Baptists will emphasize the practice of *believers' baptism*. Two key points must be made about this distinctive practice. First is the age of the baptismal candidate. The historic foundations of Baptist identity are based on our forebears' rejection of infant baptism.[5] Instead, we baptize only those persons who have made a confession of faith in Christ for themselves. The exact age at which this decision is believed possible varies widely among Baptist groups; some affirm it to be as young as age 8;

others have required candidates to reach adulthood (age 21 or, historically, even 30) before being eligible for baptism. Age 12 is a more typical age of eligibility for candidates in the twenty-first century.

The second point to emphasize regarding believers' baptism concerns the mode: full bodily immersion. In other words, Baptists do not simply sprinkle or pour water over (affuse) the head of the candidate. Instead, Baptist churches require converts to the faith to be baptized in a body of water that allows the candidate to be submerged under the water. The Greek word for baptism is *baptizo,* which carries the meaning of immerse or dip. Baptists cite Matthew 3:6, Acts 8:38, Romans 6:4, and Colossians 2:12 to support the notion that baptism should be done by immersion.

Baptists vary in the degree to which they accept as valid other modes of baptism as practiced by other Christian groups. At what age does your congregation affirm eligibility for baptism? Does your church require new members to be rebaptized if they have only been sprinkled or affused? How would you deal with a person whose infant baptism was confirmed at an older age? What if the person was immersed, but in a different denomination or at a very young age? Many Baptist churches will accept any of these candidates as full church members on the basis of their years of Christian experience, without requiring them to be baptized again by immersion or in a specific tradition.

I do not propose to settle any and all debates around the issue of rebaptism here. Rather, I am urging that, as part of the training for new deacons in your local church, you include detailed information about the age, mode, and protocols for baptism in your congregation. This is especially important since, in many Baptist churches, it is the deacons who begin the process of receiving new members into the church. Whether at the front of the sanctuary, in the initial interview, or in new member classes, deacons will need to know how to answer questions and how to explain church protocols with new members who are more and more often transferring membership from one church or denomination to another.

These broad theological questions aside, there are also practical details in which every trial deacon should be instructed. After all, deacons do not just receive new members at the rail and orient them to local church life; deacons are typically involved in the baptismal service as well, if only behind the scenes. Therefore, deacon training may encompass any or all of these responsibilities:

· Drawing water into the baptismal pool
· Instructing baptismal candidates on proper attire, timely arrival, and the questions of faith
· Providing a suitable (usually white) baptismal robe for the candidate, if appropriate
· Attending to candidates immediately before and after baptism (e.g., receiving them with a towel)
· Being positioned inside the baptistery to assist the pastor as needed
· Physically assisting candidates into and out of the baptismal pool
· Providing, laundering, and storing towels, robes, or other items used during the baptism service
· Securing and providing a baptismal certificate or other presentation gift, at the baptism service or at a later date when the candidate receives the hand of fellowship.

The Lord's Supper. This ordinance goes by many names within the universal Christian church; most notable are the Eucharist, Communion, or the Mass. As with baptism, Baptists consider the Lord's Supper to be an ordinance, not a sacrament. We believe it to be something commanded by Christ to be observed by all believers for all time. Our biblical basis for this is found in Matthew 26:26-30, Mark 14:22-26, Luke 22:14-20, and 1 Corinthians 11:23-26. The practice is intended to "commemorate the death of Christ for human redemption, and to be a perpetual memorial in his churches and to his people of his sacrifice."[6]

Because some people will come to your church from Christian traditions that believe both the elements and the partaker of those elements are changed when we share the Lord's Table, you will want your deacons' training to include some good basic information about the meaning and method of the Lord's Supper in your local church. Generally, Baptists understand the Lord's Supper only as a memorial service. We are called to "do this in remembrance" of Jesus (1 Corinthians 11:24).

Throughout history, some Baptist churches have practiced what is known as "closed Communion," meaning that they restrict the Communion table to only those "immersed believers who are members in good standing of Baptist churches."[7] In the twenty-first century, however, most Baptist churches have abandoned that practice in favor of "open Communion," which is open to any believer of any denomination who desires to share with no questions asked and no conditions set. In an open Communion service, typically the only caution comes from 1 Corinthians 11:28-29, which urges, "Examine yourselves, and only then eat of the bread and drink of the cup. For all who eat and drink without discerning the body, eat and drink judgment against themselves."

Black Baptist deacons almost always have a role connected with the Lord's Supper, before, during, and after the Communion service. In some churches they may prepare the trays of bread and wine or juice, and they may also be responsible for setting up the Communion table in whatever manner traditional to the congregation. When the Communion service begins, deacons are often called upon to minister as congregants come forward, or the deacons carry the trays throughout the congregation and pass the elements from pew to pew. Usually at least one deacon is tasked with carrying the Communion elements to other locations in the church building to administer the ordinance to members who are serving elsewhere. After the service is over, responsibility for disposing of the leftover bread and wine or juice as well as cleaning and storing the Communion ware may also fall to the deacons. Be sure to instruct trial deacons about how and when such assignments are made and what responsibilities fall upon specific deacons based on their assignment.

Having served the congregation, the deacons themselves are usually served by the senior pastor or by another member of the clergy. While ordination as a deacon typically includes the privilege of serving the Communion elements, most Baptist churches require ordination to the Christian ministry (clergy status) in order to preside at the Lord's Supper. Hence, even in churches that have itinerant pastors, the Lord's Supper is often observed only on that Sunday when an ordained member of the clergy is present.

Just as deacons often have responsibility for visitation with members who are shut-in at home or in the hospital, so they may be called upon to take Communion to those church members who cannot be present when that service is observed. This means they are expected to serve the Lord's Supper in homes, hospitals, nursing homes, hospice centers, and other such locations. Take care to instruct trial deacons on how to observe all the rules of any institution they enter for this purpose. That means discovering and honoring regulations related to visiting hours, privacy, parking, proper identification, and the rights of other patients.

Because churches differ in the frequency of observing the Lord's Supper (weekly, monthly, etc.), trial deacons should clearly understand their church's schedule and method for serving Communion. This is particularly important if the Lord's Supper is served at special events such as Watch Night, Good Friday, Easter sunrise service, and even weddings. Include instruction concerning dress code when they participate in the Lord's Supper. Do the deacons wear robes and stoles or black suits and white gloves? These may seem like small matters, but when Communion Sunday rolls around and one or more trial deacons are not properly dressed for the occasion, unnecessary confusion and distress may be the result.

Deacons and Funerals

Most churches expect deacons to be present at funeral services, and new deacons will need to be trained specifically in general and specific expectations. Are deacons required to serve at every funeral hosted by the church, or only those services for church members and their families? Does that expectation hold whether the funeral is held in the church sanctuary, at a funeral parlor, or at a cemetery or mausoleum? Does a rotation of attendance exist so that not every deacon is expected to be present at every funeral? In establishing such requirements, consider how demanding these expectations may be based on the size of your congregation and its average age.

After outlining general expectations about attendance and rotation, present trial deacons with guidelines and protocols for individual responsibilities at the service itself. Such protocols often include a dress code, formal procession, and assigned seating as a group during the service. Are deacons ever expected to serve as pall bearers? And, having attended the funeral service in the church or funeral parlor, are deacons expected to accompany the family to the graveside as well? I encourage pastors and deacon boards to consider these and other questions, and then include your church's funeral procedures as part of the training for trial deacons. Funerals are too significant an occasion to entrust to on-the-spot training.

Stewardship and Christian Education

Deacons are expected to lead by example, and that should include leadership in their financial support of the church and through ministries of Christian education. What that means exactly may vary from one church to another, but trial deacons should know exactly what is expected of them in these areas.

Not every church will place an equal emphasis on the tithing principle, but deacons should have a clear understanding of what is expected of them so far as their financial support of the church is concerned. Are they expected to tithe, and if so, is the 10 percent based on their gross or net income? To what extent does continuing status as a deacon depend on their living up to expectations related to financial stewardship? Take time in your training to establish the rationale and theology behind the principle of tithing—why God requires it of God's people and why the church needs its leaders, including (even especially) deacons, to lead by example in this area as much as any other.

A deacon's involvement in Christian education raises the same issues of expectation, commitment, and leadership by example. Most churches require deacons to participate in some kind of Christian education on a regular basis. You will want to define your expectations in this area as well. What constitutes "a regular basis"? What level of participation is required—simple attendance or also a commitment to facilitating a midweek Bible study or teaching an age-level Sunday school class? Again, in your training, clearly communicate to trial deacons both the expectation and the reason for requiring deacons to participate regularly at some level and in some form of continuing Christian education.

Many churches sponsor special workshops and forums on matters ranging from financial planning to marriage enrichment, from Baptist polity to ecumenical and interfaith dialog. While everyone would certainly benefit from such learning opportunities, will your church require that deacons be present to provide leadership or support for such events? If so, explain these expectations to trial deacons as well.

Deacons and the Benevolence Ministry

Nothing a deacon does will ever approach the actual role established in Acts 6:1-7 more than participation in the benevolence ministry of their church. A benevolence ministry involves a program or system that allows the church to provide a measure of financial or material assistance to members in distress. How that program is funded and managed varies from church to church. Some churches may not have such a program at all. However, to the extent that such a program does exist, and to the extent that deacons are expected to play a role in its operation, such matters should be outlined when trial deacons are being prepared for service.

Similarly, trial deacons should be introduced to any other committees that may exist within the life and work of the deacon board or the deacons' ministry. This may include such things as a committee that corresponds with sick and shut-in members or with other churches. In some congregations, the deacons share responsibility in the annual evaluation of the pastor and in a recommendation regarding salary and benefits increases. There may also be committees that make reports on those who share in the ordinances of Communion and baptism each month, as well as purchasing and monitoring supplies for the observance of those two ordinances.

Deacons and New Members

Every Baptist church hopes that its membership will increase numerically from year to year. That is why most pastors extend a call for Christian discipleship following the sermon each week. What a blessing when persons respond to that call and come forward to join the church. When that happens, most Baptist churches have some process by which new members are received, instructed, and presented to the congregation for a voice vote to accept them as full members of the church. Because this process frequently involves deacons, trial deacons should be trained in their role.

For example, are deacons expected to assist new candidates for membership with filling out the paperwork (e.g., name, address, contact numbers, former church, candidacy based on baptism or Christian experience)? Are the deacons responsible for conducting the initial interview with new members? If so, trial deacons will need to understand candidacy based on baptism, Christian experience, letter of transfer, restoration, watch care, and any other category recognized by your church.

Often, deacons are expected to facilitate the classes that orient new members to Christian life, Baptist history and polity, and local church life. That means new deacons should be well versed in those categories themselves. Consider making an abridged version of the new member orientation a part of trial deacon training.

When newcomers are voted into Baptist church membership, they usually receive what is known as the right hand of fellowship. This formal act of welcome into the church is traditionally led by the senior pastor and other clergy, but many churches also involve the deacons. What role, if any, do deacons in your church play in this ceremony? Does the board chair introduce new members to the congregation and make the motion to receive them as new members? Do the deacons lead the way in extending the hand of fellowship? Are they responsible for preparing certificates or gifts of presentation? Be sure to train your trial deacons not only in their specific responsibilities but in the protocols and procedures, including dress code, seating area, and receiving line. Here again, the issue is not uniformity of process from one Baptist church to another but rather the priority of instructing new deacons in their responsibilities within a particular local church.

Deacons and Other Ministries of the Church

Most persons who become deacons have been active in other areas of ministry before being chosen for this ordained position. Often their faithfulness and giftedness in those other areas initially brings them to the attention of the pastor and congregation as potential deacons. The question here is simple: Are deacons expected to limit themselves only to the work of their own board, or may they also participate in other areas of church ministry? If simultaneous service is allowed, are there any limitations concerning the type or magnitude of ministry commitments (e.g., one board but numerous committees; only ministries not active during Sunday worship service; etc.)? Knowing what, if any, of these restrictions exist will help trial deacons make an informed decision about what sacrifices they are willing to make if that is the price for becoming a deacon in your local church.

Deacons and Church Policy

Some churches have a history of vesting deacons with the authority to make decisions of policy for the church. Often this takes the form of a corporate model, where the board of deacons is the board of directors, empowered to approve every aspect of church life. Having discussed this dynamic in previous chapters, suffice to say here that an essential part of deacon training is the establishment of clear guidelines about how policy is made in your local church and what role deacons are expected to play in that process.

What is the recognized and sanctioned policy-making body of your church? Perhaps policy making is shared between the board of deacons and some other group of church officers (e.g., trustees), or it may be deemed the prerogative of the pastor. If the latter, is it expected that the deacons be consulted before the pastor takes action? Many churches have a joint board or executive committee comprised of the officers of all major church boards and auxiliaries. Are the deacons represented on such a body in your congregation? Why or why not?

Standard operating procedures being established, what happens to leadership and policy-making authority in the absence of the pastor due to extended illness, death, resignation, retirement, or dismissal from office? Do church by-laws assign any role to the deacons? If so, review those roles with trial deacons in the event that such a vacuum of leadership occurs during their term of service.

Term of Office for Deacons

Length of service is one last issue to be covered in a training program for trial deacons. Traditionally, black Baptist churches have elected their deacons for life terms, a model that offers continuity and maturity on the ministry board. Once ordained, deacons serve indefinitely with no need for reelection. In churches where a lifetime term of office is still the norm, usually some provisions are made for deacons who can no longer serve due to age or physical condition. The church may grant them honorary or emeritus status, which allows them to maintain the title of deacon but exempts them from further responsibilities of service and attendance. Similarly, a process for removing ineffective or negligent deacons is strongly recommended, whether by a vote of the other deacons, a vote of the congregation, or at the discretion of the pastor.

In the twenty-first century, many black Baptist churches have abandoned the idea of life terms for deacons. Those congregations have opted instead for three- to five-year terms of service with the possibility of being reelected to one or more successive terms. In some cases this reelection process has no limits, thus making it an altered version of the life term. The important distinction is the added accountability offered by required reelection.

Other churches have established term limits for the office of deacon. A person may be permitted to serve for two consecutive terms and then step down for a year or more before being eligible for reelection. This model for length of service offers the benefit of mandated Sabbath for the hard-working deacon and of greater opportunity for new candidates for the office. However your church handles length of service for this ministry, be sure to communicate clearly the expected period of service to new deacons.

Ordination or Installation

After completing the trial period, black Baptist deacons will typically be placed in office by one of two means. The most frequently employed is the service of ordination, which transpires through the traditional laying on of hands by all clergy and ordained deacons who are present. This tradition is based on what appears to have happened in Acts 6 when the apostles laid their hands on the seven individuals chosen by the church in Jerusalem. Historically, ordination has been understood to carry with it a lifetime appointment, as is the case with those clergy who have been ordained. However, as stated previously, unlike clergy ordination, a deacon's ordination is confined to the local church where they were set apart to serve.

The ordination service for deacons almost always features a sermon, followed by an ordination prayer, both usually delivered by a member of the clergy. Traditionally, the new deacons kneel while clergy and already established deacons lay hands on the head or shoulders of each ordinand. This ceremony completes the formal ordination process. At that time, many churches conclude the service with a presentation of a Bible and ordination certificate that bears the name of the newly ordained deacons and seal of the church that has sanctioned their selection and ordination.

The second means by which deacons are established in the black Baptist church is installation. This process has grown in popularity, especially in churches that have abandoned the idea of a lifetime appointment. What is preferred in those instances is some kind of democratic process of nomination or selection (often by the pastor), followed by majority election by the congregation or board of current deacons. The subsequent installation service serves to affirm and recognize that election or selection publicly.

An installation service might involve nothing more than offering the right hand of fellowship from the pastor and the board of deacons. Other churches prefer a more elaborate service of installation that closely resembles an ordination service with a sermon and prayer and presentation of certificate and gift. The primary difference between such an installation service and a service of ordination is the omission of the laying on of hands.

Every church will need to be clear about which mode it prefers for establishing new deacons in the office. Just be sure to prepare your trial deacons for whatever process will mark the conclusion of their training period as well as its significance for their ministry and for the congregation as a whole.

Concluding Word

I have not attempted to prescribe a required curriculum or dictate the specific content for the black Baptist church universal. Instead, this chapter was designed to highlight various aspects of ministry for the next generation of deacons. The goal is to educate those trial deacons who may be under the mistaken impression that they only need to come to church on Sunday morning, dressed in black and looking pious. That single appearance during the week is a superficial representation of the time commitment actually expected from today's deacons. The purpose of training is to prepare trial deacons for the other times, occasions, and locations when the pastor, congregation, and other deacons expect their presence and participation. The training class for trial deacons is where these expectations and requirements can be explored and embraced.

Notes

1. Two helpful resources for pastors and deacon boards are the classic *The Work of the Deacon and Deaconess, Revised Edition* by Harold Nichols (Judson Press, 1964) and *The New Life: Six Studies for Baptists,* 3rd Revised Edition by Allan R. Knight and Gordon H. Schroeder (Judson Press, 2009). The former contains practical information about the responsibilities of deacons; the latter is a convenient introduction to Baptist life and thought. Many churches use it for their new member classes.

2. S. I. Stuber, *The Illustrated Bible and Church Handbook* (New York: Association Press, 1966), 128.

3. F. L. Cross and E. A. Livingstone, *The Oxford Dictionary of the Christian Church* (New York: Oxford, 1990), 1218.

4. Edward T. Hiscox, *The Hiscox Guide for Baptist Churches* (Valley Forge, PA: Judson Press, 1964), 83.

5. In keeping with the dedication of the infant Jesus at the temple, many Baptist churches offer a service of child dedication or christening that is meant to invoke God's blessings on the baby and family until that child can make a personal decision about faith in Christ.

6. Hiscox, 95.

7. Hiscox, 92.

Chapter 5

In the Footsteps of Phoebe:
Women Deacons in the Black Baptist Church

As we continue to discuss the work of the deacon in the black Baptist church, one question remains to be considered: Is it appropriate for women to serve as deacons? This is, without a doubt, one of the most controversial issues confronting the black Baptist church today. Until the last few years, the assumption that only men could serve as deacons went unchallenged in nearly all black Baptist churches. But as the issue of women in pastoral ministry becomes more and more urgent, and as more and more black women are graduating from seminary and seeking places of service in the church, the issue of women as deacons is emerging as an equally urgent question.

Many black Baptist churches have moved forward with the ordination of women into the preaching and pastoral ministry. Yet some of these same churches remain reluctant to ordain women to serve as deacons. It is as if these churches have accepted that women may serve on the pastoral staff, but their all-male deacon boards seem content to continue excluding women from their ranks.

This practice of prohibiting women from serving as deacons is especially intriguing given the fact that women make up the overwhelming majority of most Black congregations. While we might assume that men are entirely responsible for the exclusion of women from the position of deacon, it is safe to say that such exclusion could not occur without the approval or acquiescence of women concerning the ongoing existence of an all-male deacon board. Both of these words are probably appropriate, in that some of the women in these congregations may actually *approve* of the idea that only a male can serve as a deacon, because this may be a tradition with which they have grown up and believe to be biblical. Other women may *acquiesce* to the idea of an all-male deacon board, believing such an arrangement is unlikely to change, no matter how strongly they may feel to the contrary.

Women have been prevented from entering the Roman Catholic priesthood based on a combination of biblical interpretation and an established tradition reinforced by a uniformed and universal all-male hierarchy. The exclusion of women from ordained positions in the black Baptist church is the result of a similar practice of biblical interpretation and adherence to an established tradition defended by an overwhelmingly male clergy. Yet the present arrangement in the black Baptist church would not be possible if women were not somewhat complicit in that arrangement either by their acceptance or their silence.

What Does Scripture Say about Women in Church Leadership?

Those who seek to make a biblical case for excluding women from serving as deacons tend to cite three passages written by Paul that seem to relegate women to a second-class position in the church. Some will point to verses where Paul suggests women should not be permitted to speak in the church and emphasizes that it is shameful if they do so (1 Corinthians 14:33-35). Others cite a text where women are prohibited from providing leadership in the church or from exercising any authority over men (1 Timothy 2:11-12). Some will also draw on a portion of 1 Timothy 3:8-13, which we considered in the previous chapter, and its expectation that a deacon should be "the husband of one wife," and that the wife of a deacon should be well respected. Those who point to this passage believe Paul's reference to the wives of deacons is itself sufficient proof that Paul believed only men should serve in this position. We will say more about this passage later, but let's begin by examining both 1 Corinthians 14:33-35 and 1 Timothy 2:11-12 a bit more closely.

1 Corinthians 14:33-35

There can be little doubt that churches that invoke these three New Testament passages as a basis for excluding women from the role of deacon and/or preacher are making selective use of these Scriptures. While 1 Corinthians 14:33-35 says women should be silent in church, the fact is that every black Baptist church I have ever encountered allows women to speak in church. Note that Paul did not say a woman should not be permitted "to preach" in the church; Paul said a woman should not even *speak*. The Greek word is *upotago,* which carries the sense of both silence and total submission. To say that this passage prohibits women from serving as deacons while saying nothing about other roles in which women's voices can regularly and happily be heard in every black Baptist church is to miss entirely the meaning of the key word in the passage.

If this text were to be literally interpreted and applied to the life of every local church, without regard for the original context of the passage or the subsequent shifts in the cultures from the first to the twenty-first century, then women would not be expected to be silent in the pulpit alone; they would be silent everywhere in the church. They would not be allowed to speak at church meetings, in Sunday school classes, or at midweek Bible classes. Women would not be allowed to offer their personal testimonies of the grace and goodness of God in their lives or to ask the church for prayer in the face of some problem or crisis. Those who cite 1 Corinthians 14:33-35 to resist the idea of women as deacons or preachers must also prohibit women from giving the welcome address to visitors in their local church from week to week. Women would not be allowed to read the weekly announcements regarding upcoming events in the life of the church. Not only would women be

prohibited from preaching a funeral eulogy or offering a comforting prayer, but they would also be prohibited from reading
a condolence letter from the church or one of its auxiliaries.

It is safe to say that if the men of the church forced women
to be *upotago* within the church, as some seem to desire at least
with regard to the role of deacon or preacher, the implications
on the day-to-day life of the congregation would be immediate
and serious. My experience tells me that a number of important tasks would not be accomplished in most black Baptist
churches if only men were allowed to speak. If it were not for
the leadership and creativity of women in our churches, most
of our Easter and Christmas pageants involving church youth
would never take place. Vacation Bible School would never
happen if it were left solely in the hands of the men authorized
to speak in church. If it is so urgent that men do all the talking
and teaching in the church, then why are men absent from so
many of the settings where talking and teaching take place in
the church with the single exception of the Sunday morning
worship service?

Another problem with a strict, literal understanding of this
passage concerns verse 35, which begins: "If there is anything
they desire to know, let them ask their husbands at home."
This might work in the context of the first-century Corinthian
church where the vast majority of women were married and the
vast majority of men were involved in the religious life of the
community. Today, many black women who attend church on
a regular basis are not married, and many black men are not
regularly involved in the life of the church. The reality is that
many black women have no husband at home, and in many
other homes the husband is completely cut off from the church
and, therefore, ill-equipped to serve as a spiritual guide. This
shift from male leadership in the first-century church to large-
scale male absence from the church in the twenty-first century
cannot be ignored or overlooked by those who offer this passage as justification for excluding women from leadership in
the church. In other words, in addition to being an outdated

biblical analysis, the literal application of this passage to the life
of the black Baptist church today is a practical impossibility.

1 Timothy 2:11-12

The practical problems of a literal enforcement of 1 Corinthians
14:33-35 apply equally to a literal enforcement of the words of
Paul in 1 Timothy 2:11-12: "Let a woman learn in silence with
all submission. I permit no woman to teach or to have authority over a man." Here, again, we run into the word *upotago*.
Here, again, we are forced back on the question: What black
Baptist church in the twenty-first century actually lives by that
literal understanding of the passage? As with the passage in
1 Corinthians 14, enforcement of this passage would prohibit
women not only from serving as deacons and ministers but also
from serving as chair of the Board of Trustees (or any other
church board) if that board had male members. This prohibition would also extend to the church choir or usher board if
men belonged to either of those groups.

The use of this passage to prohibit women solely from serving as deacons and ministers is clearly an abuse of the text that
is intended to buttress a certain power arrangement in which
women are excluded from any church office or position that
men do not want them to hold. If women are to be silent in
the church, then that silence cannot be limited to the two positions of deacon and preacher; it would have to extend to every
aspect of the life of the local church. *There is no black Baptist
church in America that embraces a literal enforcement of those
two Pauline passages!* In fact, few black Baptist churches in
America would survive if women were relegated to the position
suggested by a literal enforcement of these two passages.

My pastoral mentor and friend, the late William Augustus
Jones Jr., formerly of the Bethany Baptist Church of Brooklyn,
New York, had a humorous way of commenting on what he
would do if the women in his church were ever to step aside
and relinquish all their leadership roles. He said he would
move quickly to preach his departing sermon from that church,

drawing his text from the words of Paul in 2 Corinthians 13:11 (KJV): "Finally, brethren, farewell."

The Changing Status of Women

Another factor must be considered when using these two biblical texts from the first century to define what women can do in the church of the twenty-first century: The status of women in society has fundamentally changed. Women in the ancient Jewish-Greco-Roman world were not counted as citizens or as full members of society. They were a subordinated group in every sense of the word. The closest comparison might be the status of women today in conservative Islamic countries like Afghanistan or Saudi Arabia, or the behavior that would be proscribed for all Muslim women if the Taliban and other enforcers of strict Islamic law known as Sharia Law had their way. The point is clear: We cannot separate the way women in ancient cultures were forced to behave from their overall status (or non-status) in those societies.

Of course, vestiges of inequality in status between men and women remain in the United States. It cannot be forgotten that the right to vote, the ultimate sign of one's full citizenship in this country, was granted to former male slaves in 1870 through the Fifteenth Amendment to the U.S. Constitution. Yet the white female former owners of these slaves—and all other women—were not granted a similar right until the passage of the Nineteenth Amendment in 1920. Ignore for a moment that racism and terrorism were tools used to prevent black men from exercising their right to vote until the passage of the Voting Rights Act in 1965. It is still one of the great ironies of U.S. history that former black slaves were legally entitled to vote fifty years before their former female owners.

Disparities between men and women still exist in the United States in areas such as salary, upward mobility in the workplace, policies that govern maternity and paternity leave, and restrictions on the roles women in the military can play in combat situations. However, it remains crystal clear that 1 Corinthians 14:33-35 and 1 Timothy 2:11-12 address the role of women in the church at a time when society was fundamentally different than today. In ancient Israel, a woman would never have become a member of the Sanhedrin, the elite ruling assembly of that country, or one of its leading rabbinical scholars. A woman would not be considered for promotion in the ranks of the Israelite military forces nor her advice sought in the shaping of domestic or foreign policy. In that cultural context women were not to speak unless spoken to, and even then their responses had to be circumspect.

We live at a time when women serve on the U.S. Supreme Court, in both houses of Congress, as U.S. Secretary of State and U.S. Ambassador to the United Nations, as columnists for national newspapers and hosts of their own nationally syndicated TV shows. Women serve as city mayors and state governors. Women serve as corporate executives, college presidents, financial managers, professional athletes, entertainment mega-stars, and cutting-edge scholars in every field of inquiry. The role of women in society has been turned upside down from the first to the twenty-first century. If the culture that required women to be *upotago* has ended, should not the idea of women being *upotago* in the church end as well?

Phoebe and Romans 16:1-2

While those who oppose women serving as deacons are quick to cite Paul's words from 1 Corinthians 14:33-35 and 1 Timothy 2:11-12, it is interesting to note that these same pastors and church members seem to pay no attention to what Paul said in Romans 16:1-2. Here, the same Paul who is so dearly embraced by the anti-women-in-ministry crowd makes a clear reference to a woman in the church in Cenchreae named Phoebe, whom he refers to as a *diakonos*. The failure to give thorough consideration to this text is another instance of the selective reading of Scripture. This selective reading not only involves the narrow way in which certain passages are applied, but it also extends to the willingness of so many black pastors and churches to simply ignore any verse that suggests that Paul saw women as peers and equals who were qualified to hold high office in the life of the early church.

The word *diakonos,* which Paul uses to refer to Phoebe, is the same word used in 1 Timothy 3:8 and commonly translated as *deacon.* It's the same word Paul uses in Philippians 1:1 to refer to himself and Timothy. It's the same word Paul uses in 1 Timothy 4:6 when he tells Timothy how to be a good minister of Christ Jesus. It's the same word Paul uses in 1 Thessalonians 3:2 when he refers to Timothy as God's fellow worker. Again and again throughout his epistles, the great apostle refers to male leaders in the church with the exact same word he uses to describe the work of Phoebe—*diakonos.*

Paul asserts that Phoebe fulfilled the essential require-ments of a deacon. Here are his precise words; "I commend to you our sister Phoebe, a deacon (*diakonos*) of the church in Cenchreae . . . she has been a benefactor of many and of myself as well" (Romans 16:1-2, NRSV). Phoebe was a deacon in the church in Cenchrea by virtue of her service to the people and to Paul himself. (Other English Bibles translate *diakonos* here as "servant"; see the NIV and NASB.) Phoebe did what the men appointed in Acts 6 were called upon to do—she aided and assisted an apostle in the service of Jesus Christ.

There may be some people who will attempt to translate the word *diakonos* as applied to Phoebe as *deaconess.* The New International Version of the Bible, which translates the word as *servant,* includes a note suggesting the word *deaconess* as an alternate possibility. But this does not mean she was a dea-coness in the way the word has been defined traditionally in many Baptist churches, meaning a woman married to a male deacon. The word is still *diakonos*—which can only mean that Phoebe was a deacon! Even the New International Version's *Life Application Bible* states in its commentary on this verse: "Phoebe was highly regarded in the church, and she may have delivered this letter from Corinth to Rome. This provides evidence that women had important roles in the early church."[1]

Does *"Diakonos"* Apply Only to Men?

In his commentary on Romans, Joseph Fitzmyer notes that "Paul calls Phoebe *diakonos,* which may designate her generically as an 'assistant' or 'minister' in the church or specifically as a 'deacon,' a member of a special group in the church."[2] Fitzmyer acknowledges that there is some debate within scholarly circles as to whether or not Phoebe's role as a *diakonos* should be viewed as making her a member of "an order which clearly emerged in the church by the time of Ignatius of Antioch"[3] (a bishop in Syria who was martyred in AD 107). While some scholars deny that Phoebe held any official standing in the church in Cenchreae, Fitzmyer himself concludes that "it is not clear."[4]

While it is clear that the apostle Paul identifies Phoebe as a *diakonos* in the church in Cenchreae, it is unclear whether or not women served in similar positions in other churches of Asia Minor. It is also unclear whether or not women were allowed to serve in the official order that first came to be known as "deacons" in the second century AD. However, we are left with the canonical words of Romans 16:1-2 in which Paul refers to Phoebe as a *diakonos,* and urges the church in Rome to receive her in a manner worthy of the saints.

Don Williams in his book *The Apostle Paul & Women in the Church* is especially helpful when he observes that any attempt to translate or understand the term *diakonos* as "deaconess" when applied to Phoebe would be inaccurate. He states:

> Her title, deacon, is in the masculine; there are therefore no linguistic or theological grounds to distinguish between her and other male ministers. . . . There is no reason to suppose that Phoebe does not hold a ministerial office. She undoubtedly performs ministerial functions which are

equally shared by Paul and others. Thus no sexual qualifications are made here for such ministry."[5]

That point about Phoebe being considered as on par with men who are also referred to as *diakonos* is further reinforced by Evelyn and Frank Stagg when they note that "there is no term *deaconess* here (Romans 16:1-2) or elsewhere in the New Testament. Phoebe was a *deacon*."[6] The Staggs recognize the controversy that surrounds the ordination or designation of women to the office of deacon as it is understood in the contemporary church. Thus they observe, "This passage cannot be used as a proof text clinching the argument for women 'deacons,' but it is solidly on the side of acknowledging the partnership of women in the work of the church.[7]

Consensus and Uniformity Are Not the Goal

A brief survey of the literature focused on the work of the deacon in the Baptist church in general and in the black Baptist church in particular reveals a wide divergence of opinion on many important issues. There is no agreement on the precise relationship of authority between pastors and deacons. There is no agreement on whether deacons should be ordained to that office for life or whether they should be appointed to serve for a certain number of years. Even among churches that ordain deacons for life, there is some disagreement as to whether an elderly deacon can be moved from active to emeritus status. There is no consensus regarding whether a deacon must be married, whether a person who has been through a divorce can become a deacon, or whether a deacon who gets a divorce while in office should remain or be required to step down.

Similarly, black Baptist churches may continue to disagree regarding questions about ordaining women to serve in the office of deacon. The goal of this chapter is not to drive all black Baptist churches to consensus and uniformity on this issue. To the contrary, if there is room for churches to hold varying views about which men may serve as deacons, the hope here is that local churches will allow for openness and flexibility regarding women serving as deacons. The principle of autonomy, which is the absolute heart and soul of Baptist polity, says that no black Baptist church should be required to take an action simply because this is what is being done by a sister congregation. But if the ordaining of women as deacons is not contrary to biblical teachings, and if each autonomous congregation is free to make it own decisions, then churches need to seriously consider whether a continuing refusal to ordain women reflects a blatant gender bias.

The Bible Opposes Both Racism and Sexism

For the last twenty years, womanist theologians have observed that, while the black church has been aggressive in challenging the evils of racism, it has been negligent on issues of sexism and gender discrimination. Reflecting on the language of Galatians 3:28, these theologians note that virtually all black churches and black pastors welcome the idea that "In Christ there is neither slave nor free." These words were used to justify ending the evil practice of slavery that impacted black people for so many centuries solely because of their ethnicity. The same could be said about the phrase, "neither Jew nor Gentile," which represented another of the great cultural barriers that served to divide and prioritize groups of people in the ancient world.

However, when it comes to "neither male nor female for all are one in Christ Jesus," some churches and clergy seem to resist that social rearrangement. There are people who hold up passages from Paul's writings that condemn racism and classism, yet seem unwilling to embrace other passages in which Paul seems intent on moving the church forward on the issue of gender inclusion. But if we say we are guided by the Scriptures, we must not select from the text only the parts we personally agree with, while ignoring those passages that seem to point us in a direction we do not want to go.

Many individuals use a faulty understanding of certain Bible passages to support their belief that women should not hold leadership roles in the church. These individuals simply ignore or dismiss those passages that clearly speak in favor of women as leaders in the church. Demetrius Williams, an African American biblical scholar, puts the issue in perspective when he says:

> In my reading, there are no hermeneutical or exegetical grounds to use 1 Corinthians 14:33b-36 (or any passage of Scripture, for that matter) to justify the silencing and elimination of women's voices and participation in the worship service or as ordained preachers and pastors. This view is what Paul argued vehemently against. The equality of all before God in Christ is not a Pauline invention. "He found it ready at hand in one of the key moments of earliest Christianity . . . the baptismal formula in Galatians 3:27-28, where the elimination of value judgments between the sexes was eradicated. Within the Christian community male and female are equal."[8]

Some people might argue that Galatians 3:27-28 deals only with human equality before God, but not with roles and responsibilities in the life of the church. That point is strongly disputed by David Scholer, a New Testament scholar from Fuller Theological Seminary, who states: "The point is not the obliteration of God's created differences between male and female, but is that sexual differentiation does not determine the participation in God's church for persons created in the image of God."[9]

Demetrius Williams insists that the Bible cannot be used to condemn racism yet cited in support of sexism. The Bible condemns both. Thus, Williams writes: "African American churches can no longer advocate racial equality on biblical grounds and at the same time support sexism in the churches using the same Bible. They must have the courage to judge a person by the content of his or her character and abilities, especially in the church."[10]

In his book *Speak Until Justice Wakes,* J. Alfred Smith Sr. adds another biblical text that can be used in support of women serving as preachers and deacons in the church. He points to Huldah the prophetess in 1 Kings 22:14-20, who interpreted to King Josiah the meaning of the book that had been found in the temple in Jerusalem in the seventh century BC. Over and over again, Huldah declares to King Josiah, "This is what the LORD says." Why do those who oppose women speaking or serving as spiritual leaders in the black Baptist church never talk about Huldah? I agree with Smith when he states: "If the prophetic proclamation of the woman prophet Huldah could inaugurate reform and revival in Judah, what could prophetic preaching by women accomplish in America and in the world today? I say let Huldah speak for God today."[11]

The Bible Has Been Used to Oppress

Many black Christians are aware that the passage in Romans 13 about "being subject to the governing authorities" was used by slave owners for more than 200 years to provide a biblical justification for slavery. Howard Thurman once reported that, when he was asked to read the Bible to his grandmother who had lived as a slave in Florida, she ordered him to skip over many passages that had been used to justify slavery.[12] The Bible was regularly used to exclude black people from certain aspects of life in American society. There is no black person who wants to return to a time when the Bible was read and interpreted in ways that perpetuated their continued exploitation and exclusion.

Yet many within the black Baptist church are using the Bible as the basis upon which we argue that our own black women should be excluded from certain positions within the life of the church solely on the basis of their gender. We know the Bible says "in Christ there is neither male nor female," but we suggest that verse refers to equal worth as humans, but not to equal roles within the church. We know about Phoebe in Romans 16:1-2, but we want to insist she was a deaconess in the modern sense of that word even though the word *diakonos* is used to refer to men throughout the writings of Paul.

The Bible Is Not the Obstacle

Again, my objective in this chapter is not to resolve the question of whether or not women should serve as deacons in the black Baptist church. My objective is to suggest that there are no biblical prohibitions against woman serving in that office. The passages used to prohibit women from serving as deacons or preachers have been torturously misinterpreted and selectively applied by most black pastors and churches. It is incomprehensible that Paul's instruction to twenty-first century churches is that women should be silent, submissive, and subordinated to roles that never allow them to teach or have authority over males. The day women stop speaking, teaching, leading, and providing essential support for their local churches is the day those churches will very likely go out of business.

Women are not excluded from the offices of deacon and preacher in most black Baptist churches because of our accurate adherence to biblical teaching. The primary reason for excluding women is gender discrimination—something that can no more be supported or defended through the use Scripture than the racial discrimination so long directed against black people in the United States.

In addressing the question of women as deacons in the black Baptist church, I want to shift the focus to the experience of one particular congregation, the Antioch Baptist Church of Cleveland, Ohio, where I have served as the pastor since 1987. I want to share the story of our process in deciding to elect and ordain women to be deacons, a practice we began in 1997. As the study moves into the next chapter, I want to present the model our congregation used in its process, a model I hope will prove to be helpful as more and more churches move in the direction of electing and ordaning women to be deacons.

Notes

1. *The Life Application Study Bible,* The New International Version, Romans 16:1-2 notes (Wheaton: Tyndale House Publishers, 1991), 2438–39.

2. Joseph Fitzmyer, *Romans,* The Anchor Bible #33 (New York: Doubleday, 1992), 729.

3. Fitzmyer, 729.

4. Fitzmyer, 729.

5. Don Williams, *The Apostle Paul & Women in the Church* (Glendale, CA: Regal Books, 1977), 42–43.

6. Evelyn and Frank Stagg, *Women in the World of Jesus* (Philadelphia: Westminster Press, 1978), 180.

7. Evelyn and Frank Stagg, 180.

8. Demetrius K. Williams, *An End to This Strife: The Politics of Gender in African American Churches* (Minneapolis: Fortress Press, 2004), 71.

9. David M. Scholer, "A Biblical Basis for Equal Partnership: Women and Men in the Ministry of the Church" (Valley Forge, PA: American Baptist Women in Ministry, 1997), 7.

10. Demetrius K. Williams, 71.

11. J. Alfred Smith Sr., *Speak Until Justice Wakes* (Valley Forge, PA: Judson Press, 2006), 55.

12. Howard Thurman, *Jesus and the Disinherited* (Boston: Beacon Press, 1996), 30.

Chapter 6

How One Church Embraced Women in Ordained Ministry

In addressing the question of women as deacons in the black Baptist church the focus now shifts to an examination of how one church worked through the process of deciding to elect and ordain women to be deacons. Here, I will be sharing the story of Antioch Baptist Church in Cleveland, Ohio, where I have served as pastor since 1987. While understanding that every congregation is free to organize itself as it sees fit within the boundaries of biblical doctrine and Baptist polity, I hope that our congregation's experience will prove helpful as more and more churches move in the direction of women deacons.

Antioch Baptist Church ordained a woman to be a deacon for the first time in 1997. Since then, six other women have joined her as deacons in this church. These seven women are not called or considered deaconesses, which in most black Baptist churches is either a title given to the wife of a male deacon or an honorific title assigned to a woman in recognition of her "servant's heart." Our congregation includes women who serve as deaconesses in both of the above named capacities. However, the seven women who serve as deacons are not considered a part of those groups.

These seven women deacons sit with and serve alongside their male counterparts. They help prepare candidates for baptism. They assist in preparing and serving Holy Communion. They aid in interviewing candidates for benevolence support from the church (*waiting on tables*). They visit the members of the congregation at home and in the hospital. They serve as worship leaders on Sunday mornings and during other occasions such as revivals and seasonal celebrations. They attend and have voting privileges at meetings of the Board of Deacons and they are eligible to hold any office on that board. These women are, in every way, deacons of Antioch Baptist Church.

The decision to ordain women to serve as deacons in the Antioch Baptist Church of Cleveland, Ohio, came as a result of a very intense and deliberate process. It was not done against the will of the congregation or over the objections of the existing all-male deacon board. It was also not done by the sole authority of the pastor, as happens in some churches. Rather, it was approved at a congregational meeting after the matter had been discussed for many months. In the end the debate was not whether women should be allowed to serve on the Board of Deacons. Instead, the discussion involved who our first female deacon would be.

Several names were put forward for consideration. As pastor, I joined the active members of the board in considering each name carefully. We used the language of Acts 6:3 (NKJV) that speaks about persons "of good reputation, full of the Holy Spirit and wisdom." We also used the language of 1 Timothy 3:8-9 that says, "Deacons must be reverent, not double-tongued, not given to much wine, not greedy for money, holding the mystery of the faith with a pure conscience" (NKJV). Many women in the church met those qualifications, yet there was an intentional decision to begin with one exemplary candidate who would be readily elected by the church and who would also perform in a way that would open the door for the other women we hoped would follow after her.

In other words, we started slow out of an awareness that ordaining a woman as deacon was not just something new for Antioch Baptist Church; it was something that had been done by no other black Baptist church in Cleveland at that time. When we made this decision in 1997, we were the first black

Baptist church in our city ever to take this step, and we were not sure how many women had been ordained and appointed to serve as deacons in black Baptist churches anywhere else in the country. However, we were less interested in making history than in making sure the first woman we ordained to be a deacon would be a catalyst for the others who would want to follow after her.

The Jackie Robinson Model

As we considered who would be ordained as our church's first woman deacon, we reflected on the story of Jackie Robinson, who in 1947 became the first black person to play Major League Baseball in the modern era. It has been widely observed that Jackie Robinson was not the best player in the Negro Leagues, but Branch Rickey, the owner and general manager of the Brooklyn Dodgers, was looking for more than on-field talent. He was also looking for a person of impeccable off-field reputation. Rickey was looking for someone whose morals could not be challenged, whose patriotism could not be questioned, and whose character was beyond reproach.

When he signed Jackie Robinson to a contract in 1946, Branch Rickey knew he was getting more than an excellent baseball player. He was getting a college graduate from UCLA. He was getting an All-American athlete in both football and baseball. He was getting a military veteran who achieved officer rank. He was getting someone who was engaged to be married before the 1947 season would begin. Rickey knew that signing a black man to play Major League Baseball would be a controversial act. He wanted to choose someone about whom the only objection could be his race, because the rest of his life was admirable in every way.

Our decision to ordain a woman to become a deacon was informed by a similar philosophy. We were looking not only for someone who met all the biblical standards, but also for someone whose public life and Christian service in the church was so exemplary that *the only grounds upon which anyone could oppose her selection and ordination was that she was a woman.* Once our candidate had been selected and presented to the church, and once the actual intentions of certain biblical passages had been addressed and resolved, the road was cleared to add our first woman to the board of deacons.

It should be noted that Antioch Baptist Church did not begin the process of including women in leadership roles with the ordination of Dorothy Rambo as a deacon in 1997. Our work actually began a full decade earlier, when Tonya Fields was ordained and then hired to a full-time position on the ministerial staff of our church. Two other women have subsequently been ordained to the preaching ministry of our congregation. Since 1987, a total of ten women have now been ordained as either ministers or deacons of our church. Their presence and participation has been a blessing to me and to our congregation.

Our congregation's experience in ordaining women ministers since 1987 and women deacons since 1997 can be a blessing to other congregations that may be open to the idea. We believe men and women should be considered equally when it comes to filling the two biblical offices of preacher and deacon. We were intentional in starting with the ordination of women to the pastoral ministry, believing that to be the bigger and more challenging step. If women could be accepted as presiders at the communion table alongside their male ministerial colleagues, surely there could be no objection if women distributed the elements alongside male deacons. If women could be embraced as they preached the gospel from the pulpit, surely there would be no difficulty with their leading prayers, visiting the sick, or helping shape the policies by which the church is governed.

The Status of Black Men Has Changed

When the discussion first began about the possibility of ordaining women to become deacons in a black Baptist church, there was a keen awareness of the historic importance of the office of deacon in the black Baptist church. We understood that our actions were breaking with a long-standing precedent which held that the board of deacons was a "male only" preserve. We knew all our members had grown up in churches where a woman had never served as an ordained deacon. We carefully considered the fact that there would be sister congregations right here in Cleveland that not only would refuse to follow our example but also would likely refuse to recognize the status of our women deacons.

We also understood that there was a time when the office of deacon in the church provided one of the very few opportunities for black males to enjoy a position of prominence and influence in U.S. society. We knew there had been a time when black men who were sharecroppers, chauffeurs, landscapers, Pullman porters, or manual laborers during the week could look ahead to Sunday morning when they would walk into their home church and be greeted not as "boy" or "uncle," but instead greeted as "Deacon." We understood that being a deacon in the church was once one of the few ways that the self-esteem of black men could be lifted in a society that used every available opportunity to debase, humiliate, and sometimes even emasculate black men.

However, in 1997, as we considered the possibility of ordaining women to become deacons, it seemed to us that those historic arguments no longer carried as much weight as they once did. While the evils of racism and discrimination persist, black men as a group are not unilaterally denied opportunities within the wider American society. Black men do not need to look upon service on the local church's board of deacons as a way to offset the lack of opportunity for education, employment, and advancement that earlier generations may have faced.

In fact, anyone who attempts to make the argument that the board of deacons in a black Baptist church should remain an all-male setting so that black men have at least one place where they are given the opportunities to serve in a leadership role would be ignored or dismissed as being sadly out of touch with how far our society has come in the last fifty years. If a black man named Barack Obama can now live in the White House, it can no longer be said that the office of deacon in the black church must be restricted to male candidates because they are unable to enjoy opportunity elsewhere. Black men occupy positions of power, authority, and influence at every level throughout American society. It should be added that their presence is not limited to a handful of athletes and entertainers, but includes leaders in the fields of education, business, politics, publishing, TV and radio broadcasting, and the sciences.

It is time to put to rest, once and for all, the notion that women should not serve as deacons or preachers in the black Baptist church because those are among the very few positions in society where a black man can enjoy authority and influence. More importantly, if the role of a deacon is to serve the community or to "wait on tables" (as has been argued throughout this study), then reserving this position for men so they can enjoy power and influence entirely misses the point of what it means to be a deacon!

It is worth mentioning that it is whispered in some church circles that female opposition to women serving in church leadership positions is the primary stumbling block for many churches. I have found no data or research to support that claim; but it at least needs to be acknowledged as one of the arguments set forward by some. Most black Baptist churches are comprised primarily of women; and many of those women are unmarried women with children. It is sometimes argued that women in this situation look to the pastor and deacons for more than spiritual leadership and direction; they look to them as surrogate husbands for themselves and surrogate fathers for their children. Obviously, these are expectations that women serving in these same positions could not fill.

Yet we must take great care not to impose roles or responsibilities on deacons or pastors in the black Baptist church that were never set forth by the Bible. We cannot let the selection of who can and cannot serve as a deacon in the church hang on any dismal statistics that may be reported on the state of marriage and two-parent households in the black community. Moreover, if other black denominations do not use that as a basis for refusing to ordain women into leadership positions then it should also hold no special weight with black Baptists.

Many Still Resist on Biblical Grounds

No matter how many examples are presented about the changing status of both black men and black women in society, no matter how much information is presented about the context for Paul's writings about the role of women or his designation of Phoebe as a deacon, there will continue to be many people who believe the Bible itself supports their claim that women cannot serve as deacons in the church. They will continue to point to the two isolated passages from Paul that they believe speak against the practice of women serving in any ordained leadership position in the church. In fact, they will state that they are upholding Scripture by resisting the social and cultural influences that are infusing their way into the life of the church. This is especially true within the black Baptist church, even in the face of the advances enjoyed by women in so many areas and arenas outside of the church.

The belief that the Bible opposes women in any leadership position in the church continues to hold sway in some black Baptist churches. There are still churches where women cannot stand behind the pulpit for any reason. When women address the congregation, they must speak from a side lectern or stand on the floor. There are even some churches where women cannot speak in the sanctuary at all. The folly of this position is that the biblical texts make no reference as to where in the sanctuary a woman should stand when she speaks in and to the church. The first-century practice Paul was suggesting was that women should not speak in the church at all (*upotago*)! Some black Baptist churches may allow women to function as unordained local missionaries or unofficial evangelists who "speak" at women's conferences or on Women's Day in the church, but these women are not allowed to sit in the pulpit area with male clergy. They are never considered when discussion about ordaining new deacons comes up.

Many black women have left Baptist churches in frustration, hoping that their aspirations to serve God as an ordained minister can be fulfilled within another denomination. Although there was a time when virtually all black denominations prohibited women from serving in an ordained position, this is no longer the case. Black Methodists have all moved beyond their earlier resistance to the idea of women serving in leadership positions in their churches. In 1809 Richard Allen of the African Methodist Episcopal Church refused to ordain Jarena Lee, telling her that "our Discipline knew nothing at all about it—that it did not call for women preachers."[1] Yet the AME Church and the AME Zion Church both have female bishops, and all three historically black Methodist churches including the Christian Methodist Episcopal Church have females serving as elders (pastors) in their churches.

Be Prepared for the Consequences

When we made the decision to ordain women as preachers and deacons at Antioch Baptist Church in Cleveland, we knew our actions would be met with negative reactions from some other churches in our city. In the black Baptist church tradition there are frequent occasions when two or more congregations gather to worship together, such as on church anniversaries, Good Friday, Easter, Christmas Eve, or New Year's Eve. The normal practice at such services has deacons from each participating church gather at the front of the sanctuary to lead the congregation in a devotional service before the actual order of worship begins. We knew some churches in our community would not allow a woman deacon to participate in that important and highly visible ministry. We knew our women deacons would be openly criticized for refusing to "stay in their place." It quickly became our church policy to avoid entering into congregational fellowship with any other congregation that would not welcome "all our deacons."

None of this came as a surprise to us when we ordained our first woman deacon, because we had already experienced the consequences of breaking with the precedent of ordaining only men when we ordained our first woman to the Christian ministry. She served faithfully and effectively with us for seven years, and then sought to move into a new ministry as senior pastor of a congregation. Despite the number of black Baptist churches in the region that were searching for a pastor at that time (1994–95), and despite her excellent service with us as both a preacher and a teacher of the gospel, not one of those black Baptist churches was willing to consider her for the position. Ultimately, she ended up affiliating with the United Methodist Church in order to pursue the ministry to which both she and we believe she has been called.

It was both heartening and heartbreaking to discover that other churches that proceeded with the ordination of women as deacons and clergy have had similar experiences. One of my clergy colleagues speaks movingly of the profound sense of loneliness and isolation that resulted from his church's decision to ordain women to these positions. Male clergy who support the ordination of women as deacons and preachers are undoubtedly doing the right thing, but doing the right thing has often come with negative consequences.

It should not be forgotten that something similar happened when many white denominations proceeded with the designation and ordination of black people as lay leaders, pastors, and denominational officials. How sad that some black people, who have themselves been excluded and scorned because of a skewed reading of select biblical verses, now practice a similar selective reading themselves in an attempt to block women from ordained leadership roles in the church.

Avoiding the Easy Road

There were many points along the way to that first ordination when we could have turned back to the familiar tradition of an all-male board of deacons. We could have taken the approach that racists within white society advocated regarding racial integration: "The time is not yet right. Let's wait a little longer." We could also have taken another favorite, though disingenuous, approach of white society and stated that we could not find "any qualified candidates." However, while the status quo may seem like the safest place for a local church to stand on this issue, it may, in fact, be the most cowardly and ungodly place for the followers of Christ to find themselves.

The words of Dante's *Inferno,* so often quoted by Dr. Martin Luther King Jr. during the Civil Rights Movement, also apply as our society considers the inclusion of women in roles and offices once unavailable to them solely because of their gender. Dante said, "The hottest place in hell is reserved for those persons who, in the time of choosing, cling to neutrality." Our congregation believed then, and we believe even more firmly today that, "In Christ there is neither male nor female" (Galatians 3:28). We believed then and we believe even more firmly today that there are no offices, duties, or responsibilities within the life of a local Baptist church that are restricted only to men. We believed then and we believe even more firmly today that when Paul made reference to Phoebe as a deacon (*diakonos*) in Romans 16:1-2 he was providing the biblical authority we needed to proceed with the ordination of a woman as a deacon in our church.

This chapter was based largely on our experiences at Antioch Baptist Church in Cleveland, Ohio. While our church's story is important, it goes without saying that the experiences of a single autonomous congregation cannot provide the basis for legitimate conclusions or a consensus of opinion about this controversial issue. In order to offer a broader and more objective discussion about women as deacons, as well as other recent developments in the role and responsibilities of deacons in the twenty-first century, a survey was prepared and administered to a cross-section of pastors in the Greater Cleveland area as well as several other regions across the country. The insights raised by the responses to that survey will provide the substance of our next chapter.

Note

1. Jarena Lee, "A Female Preacher among the African Methodists," in *African American Religious History: A Documentary Witness,* edited by Milton C. Sernett (Durham: Duke University Press, 1999), 173.

Chapter 7

A Twenty-first Century Look at a First Century Ministry

It has been asserted throughout this study that the primary role of the deacon in the black Baptist church today remains the same as in the in the first century when the office of the deacon was created: Deacons are to serve the local church. While the essence of the deacon's role remains unchanged, it is not surprising that there have been changes and shifts in the specific forms by which that service is offered. Today's black church is not a communal organization in which all members have pooled their financial resources into a common pool overseen and distributed by the deacons. Instead, most black Baptist churches operate on the tithes and offerings of the members of each congregation. In most cases those funds are collected, counted, deposited, spent, and reported on by trustees who are not members of the deacon board and do not report to or answer to the deacons.

In light of that fundamental change from the first to the twenty-first century, we are left with the question of what duties are required of the deacons in today's church. What is the modern equivalent of "waiting on tables"? If the black Baptist church of today no longer requires deacons to oversee a common fund, what other tasks are in keeping with that same spirit of service today? And what are the qualifications for the persons who will serve in this role in today's black Baptist church?

How should they be selected? How long should they serve in that position?

Waiting on Tables in the Twenty-first Century

In an attempt to better define the role and responsibilities of deacons in the black Baptist church, a survey was conducted in 2008–09. The survey invited pastors to answer a series of questions about the role and function of deacons in the congregations they were serving currently. The survey was designed to create a database of information about the work of the deacon in the black Baptist church and included questions on a range of topics including how deacons are selected, what roles they perform, and how long they are allowed to remain in office. Questions also sought to discover who was or was not eligible to serve as a deacon in any given church—considering factors such as age, gender, ethnicity, criminal background, marital status, and years of membership in the congregation. A copy of the full survey can be found in Appendix A.

Initially, the survey involved pastors from twenty randomly selected black Baptist congregations in the Greater Cleveland area. For purposes of regional balance, the survey was then extended to twelve pastors in San Antonio, Texas, who belong to a group called Community of Churches for Social Action. Finally, the survey was taken by twelve additional pastors from other parts of the country—ranging from Michigan to Texas, from South Carolina to Northern California, and from Georgia in the Deep South to Connecticut in New England.[1]

All told, the survey results include responses from forty-four black Baptist pastors, male and female. In order to qualify for participation in the survey, each congregation had to have a membership where African Americans constituted the clear majority. Every church surveyed was either a member of a historically black Baptist denomination or a member congregation of the multicultural American Baptist Churches USA.[2]

It must be remembered that the black Baptist church, like all Baptist churches, clings to the principle of the autonomy of the local church. That means that each congregation is free to govern and organize itself as it sees fit without having to conform or be answerable to what happens in any other Baptist congregation, or to any hierarchical or supervisory structure outside the ranks of the congregation. With that in mind, the results of this survey should not be understood as prescriptive of the role and responsibilities of deacons in any other autonomous congregation. Yet the survey itself, and the compiled responses to it, can be used by any Baptist church as it seeks guidance and direction concerning who it will consider as a potential deacon and what it may expect its deacons to do when they enter into that office.

Notable Results from the Survey

There were several aspects of the survey that were noteworthy and instructive so far as the role of the deacon in the black Baptist church is concerned. (The complete results of the survey can found in Appendix B.)

The first result worth noting was that a number of churches are moving away from the concept of a deacons' board (with an implied emphasis on administration and oversight) in favor of a deacons' *ministry* that emphasizes service to the church and assistance to the pastor. Our survey found seven churches that have made this shift. Two other churches no longer employ the term *deacon* to describe their lay leadership. One of these churches now operates with a "board of ministry" that combines the work of deacons and trustees into a single ministry. The other refers to its lay leaders as "elders." These terms are used instead of *deacon* even though these lay leaders are involved in the same tasks as those performed by deacons in other black Baptist churches. In these two churches, as in those churches that have moved from a deacon board to a deacons' ministry, the objective was to shift from an emphasis on

A Twenty-first Century Look
at a First Century Ministry

105 °

administration and oversight tasks to a service-oriented focus.
This is a significant issue even for those churches who continue
to use the term *board of deacons* yet want to make it clear that
the deacon's role is a service to the church and not supervision of
the pastor.

There is a clear tendency for churches to require new deacons to serve in a period of training ranging from one year to
eighteen months before they can be ordained into this position.
The training itself ranged from serving alongside established
deacons to learn the procedures of the particular church to an
intense period of study followed by an examination on matters
of church doctrine, Baptist polity, and biblical knowledge. As
one pastor observed, "There are only two ordained offices in
the church: preachers and deacons. We would not think about
ordaining a preacher without finding out how much he or she
knows. Why should it be any different with a deacon?"

It was surprising to discover who was and was not eligible to
serve as a deacon in the various churches surveyed. The varia-
tions stretched not only across geographic lines but also across
lines of biblical and theological difference on many questions
of church leadership. Most churches do not prohibit divorced
persons from becoming deacons, nor would the church remove
a seated deacon from the position because of a divorce. Slightly
less than half of the churches have no stated prohibition against
women serving as deacons, but only seven of the twenty-one
churches that do not prohibit women from serving as a deacon
have women serving in that capacity currently. There were no
churches that would prohibit someone who was not African
American from serving as a deacon, but only two churches had
such a person serving as a deacon at the present time.

Only one church responded that it would allow an openly
gay or lesbian person to serve as a deacon. Three other churches
responded by saying the issue had never come up in their congregations and they neither embraced nor rejected the possibility.
The fact that most churches in this survey do not allow openly
gay or lesbian persons to serve as deacons does not necessarily

mean that no one serving as a deacon in any of these churches is gay. It is quite possible that there are gay or lesbian persons who are serving as deacons in many churches, yet these individuals are not open about their sexuality or same-sex relationships. It is the black Baptist church version of "don't ask, don't tell."

There were only five churches that would prohibit anyone with a felony record from serving as a deacon. Most churches were inclined to think in terms of restoration, forgiveness, and a second chance once an individual had paid his or her debt to society. The only exceptions noted were if the crime of record was a sex offense, in which case a lifetime prohibition seemed more likely.

It was revealed that eleven of the forty-four churches have moved away from the idea of deacons serving for life, preferring that they serve for set periods of time, after which they may either be reelected or automatically rotated off the board. Thirty churches require a rotation of officers on the deacon board so that no one could be chairman of that board as a lifetime appointment. Regular elections and mandatory rotations are becoming the norm for board officers. Very few churches allow someone who has not previously served in some other position in their church to become a deacon. However, most churches allow ordained deacons to continue to serve with other auxiliaries.

Not surprisingly, all churches agreed that deacons should be involved in the Lord's Supper, and all but one expect deacons to be involved in baptisms. Similarly, every church but one expects deacons to visit members of the congregation who are sick at home or in a hospital. Most churches expect deacons to be involved, either as a teacher or a student, in some form of Christian education. All churches include the deacons in welcoming new members into the church, and the majority of churches also include deacons in new member orientation.

Only six of the forty-four churches in the survey involve deacons in overseeing the finances of the church. This goes a long way toward debunking the idea that deacons "run the church," since the majority of deacons have no hand in the counting, banking, or spending of church finances. Most churches grant the pastor a large role in determining who can become a deacon, and many of the pastors surveyed have either blocked someone from becoming a deacon or took action to remove from the position a person whose service was not up to what was expected. Most churches suggested that the pastor and deacons enjoy a positive working relationship in which each appreciates and affirms the other's work.

Churches reported that the relationship between pastor and deacons worked best when they met together on a regular basis (monthly) on ministry matters and when they prayed together (weekly) before Sunday morning worship. Problems arose when deacons were consistently looking for ways to attack, criticize, undermine, or end the leadership role of the pastor. The same could be said of situations where the pastor assumed an adversarial role toward the deacons and sought to ignore or circumvent them even on matters where their involvement and counsel might have made a positive difference.

The Duties of Deacons in the Twenty-first Century

Based upon responses to the survey questions and the written and oral comments that accompanied them, we can create a sampling of the duties expected of deacons in the black Baptist church today. In every case, these duties fulfill the purpose of serving the needs of the church while freeing the pastors to dedicate more time to preaching and prayer.

Devotional Preludes

In most black Baptist churches deacons play a role in all devotional periods that precede regular worship services as well as special gathering of the worshipping community. This would include Sunday morning and vesper services, revival meetings, and seasonal celebrations such as Advent/Christmas and Holy Week/Easter. In this role the deacons lead the congregation in prayer, hymn singing, and the sharing of personal testimonies.

These devotional services that precede the regular worship serve the purpose of "warming up" the congregation for the preaching and music that will follow, and typically last 10 to 15 minutes.

Preparatory Prayer

It is useful for deacons to meet with the pastor each Sunday morning prior to the start of that devotional service for the purpose of praying with and for the pastor as he or she prepares to deliver the sermon and to lead the congregation in worship. While those four or five minutes might also provide an opportunity to share announcements and answer a few questions about activities in and around the church, the primary purpose of this pre-worship gathering is prayer. There might even be an opportunity to sing a verse or a refrain from a popular hymn or praise song. This gathering aids and assists both the pastor and the deacons in preparing to enter the sanctuary on any given Sunday morning with their hearts and minds focused on the worship of God.

Sunday Worship

Deacons often participate in the worship service itself. In addition to being prominently seated as a group at the front of the sanctuary, individual deacons may be called upon to lead in prayer, read Scripture, assist the pastor in the pulpit, accompany the pastor in receiving any person who might come forward to join the church, or play some role during the gathering of the weekly tithes and offerings.

Midweek Services

Deacons should participate in any midweek services the local church may have, regardless of whether that service is a Bible study, a prayer meeting, a time of testimonies and bearing one another's burdens, or a full-blown worship service with a choir and preaching. The midweek service offers deacons another opportunity to provide spiritual leadership as they lead in prayer, read Scripture, and give their support to what is going on each week. These services may also allow deacons to give special attention to the names and conditions of persons who are sick or shut-in.

Christian Education

Deacons should actively participate in the Christian education offerings the local church provides. There are several reasons this is important. First, deacons should always take advantage of opportunities to increase their own knowledge of the Bible and Christian doctrine. Second, those deacons with the ability to teach should be willing to serve in the Christian education programs of the church. Third, their presence at such events allows deacons to better grasp the spiritual maturity of the congregation. This knowledge can allow them to work with the pastor or assigned clergy to strengthen that area of the church's ministry.

Right Hand of Fellowship

Deacons typically share in the ritual known as the right hand of fellowship, which is extended to all persons who join the church by the traditional methods of baptism, Christian experience, restoration, or transfer. During this ritual, the clergy and deacons receive new members into the church by welcoming each new member with a handshake. It is a joyful time of celebration when new members are welcomed into the church family. In some instances the deacons will present each new member with a Bible, a membership certificate, and/or a box of giving envelopes.

Baptism

Deacons assist in the ordinance of baptism by helping candidates dress in the appropriate gown or other baptismal clothing and assisting them in getting in and out of the waters being used for baptism. In some instances a deacon may even enter the baptismal pool or stand with the pastor in a stream or pond to assist in baptizing the candidates. In some churches the deacons play a leading role in providing baptismal candidates with some training in Christian doctrine as well as some orientation to the structure and operation of that church.

Communion Service

Deacons assist in preparing and serving the Lord's Supper both to those in the Sunday worship service as well as to members who are sick or shut-in. Most black Baptist churches employ Communion trays with bread and individual cups, often using prepackaged bread and juice. A few black Baptist churches employ a common cup where everyone drinks the wine or juice from the same cup, or dips bread into a common cup. The deacons set the Communion table, fill the cups and trays, circulate throughout the church to serve the congregation, and collect the cups at the end of the service. Deacons are also expected to serve Communion to members of the congregation who are unable to attend church due to sickness or incapacitation. It is a special blessing when deacons enter a hospital room or a nursing home to allow a member of the church to share in the ordinance of Communion.

Visitation

Deacons should make hospital and house calls on church members who are sick and shut-in. This is usually done according to a schedule or a list of church members assigned to each deacon. A good rule of thumb is to assign twenty-five members to each deacon. That deacon is expected to pay special attention to those members and respond to their needs when they are in the hospital or facing another hardship or emergency. The pastor may also visit members who are hospitalized, but deacons can relieve the work of the pastor by assuming responsibility for church members who are home-bound due to their physical condition or facing long-term convalescence.

Benevolence

Deacons should establish some arrangement for discovering
and addressing the benevolence needs of the congregation. A
fund should be established that allows deacons to respond when
members of the church are facing difficulty affording medica-
tions, providing adequate food for themselves and their families, the pending loss of essential utilities like heat and lights,
and other short-term needs. This comes close to the initial task
assigned to the seven men selected in Acts 6. In the absence of
a common fund from which all could draw, the congregation
may want to establish a policy of setting aside 2–5 percent of
the weekly tithes and offerings to be used in this manner.

Administrative Accountability

Deacons should hold periodic meetings focused on holding one
another accountable for the work they all should be doing.
Reports should be given on the home and hospital calls each
deacon has made, and reminders should be given regarding
upcoming events where the presence and participation of the
deacons is either welcome or expected. Obviously the pastor
should be made aware of such meetings so that he or she can
bring before the deacons any concerns regarding their work
or the life of the congregation. Deacons should not meet in an
attempt to determine what other church auxiliaries should or
should not do. Deacons should meet so they can all be sure they
are doing the work that has been expected of them since those
seven individuals were identified in Acts 6.

Congregational Policy-making

Deacons should have some involvement in shaping the policies of the congregation. This usually occurs when deacons
serve with other congregational leaders in the context of a
joint board, general board, or executive committee. In some
churches every deacon also serves on this joint board. In other

cases, participation is limited to three or four deacons who are either the officers of this board or who have been selected by the deacons to represent their concerns in this congregational setting.

Church Meetings

Deacons should attend all congregational meetings in which new policy and program initiatives are being discussed and adopted. It is always good to have as many deacons as possible present at church-wide congregational meetings. It signals not only the deacons' interest in what is going on, but also their general support for the policies and programs being discussed. Any deacon who wants a hand in running the church should see these joint board and congregational meetings as the appropriate time and place to make his or her voice heard and opinions known. Of course, other voices and opinions will also be heard—as they should be within an autonomous Baptist church, where all authority ultimately resides with the congregation.

Leadership Development and Discernment

Some churches grant deacons a leading role in the process of nominating and screening persons who will later be voted on for various positions in the life of the congregation. Most churches have a nominating committee on which deacons serve alongside other church members who have been elected by the congregation for this task. The participation of deacons on such a committee can be especially useful because deacons who have been assigned to stay in close contact with twenty-five members of the congregation will have a good sense of which people are most active in the life of the church.

Many churches grant deacons the opportunity to nominate other persons to serve alongside them as deacons. It is unusual for any church to grant existing deacons sole authority to select who will be added to their ranks. It is most common for nominations to be approved by the pastor and then voted on by the congregation so new deacons will be serving with the widest possible endorsement and affirmation. Some churches allow the pastor to directly appoint people to become deacons. As always, each Baptist church has the right to govern itself as it sees fit!

Funeral Services

Most churches expect deacons to attend funeral services for members of the church. This can pose some difficulty for deacons with full-time jobs who are members of larger churches that may average twenty-five or thirty funerals each year. That makes it all the more important that those deacons who are retired from full-time employment make the effort to be present as often as possible. The presence of both deacons and clergy is a great comfort to the bereaved family and a genuine sign of respect for the deceased member.

Community Services

It is quite common in the black Baptist tradition for two or more congregations to share in a service in observance of some special occasion in the life of one or more of those churches. The occasions may include a church anniversary, a pastoral anniversary, or an annual day hosted by one of the auxiliaries of the church. Deacons should make an effort to be present when their church is hosting such an event. It is even more important that deacons travel with the pastor when he or she is invited to preach at a sister congregation for one of these services. No pastor wants to accept the invitation to preach at another church, arrive at the location, and have none of the deacons of his or her own church seated in the congregation.

Interim Leadership

Deacons often play a significantly larger role in the life of a local church during those times when the pastor is incapacitated or when the church has no pastor due to resignation, retirement, dismissal, or death. Under those circumstances the congregation often turns to the deacons to sustain the work of the church until the current pastor returns or a new pastor is chosen. In addition to finding preachers to fill the pulpit each week, deacons may also be expected to lead the efforts of a search committee as it identifies and screens prospective candidates for the pastoral position.

Spiritual Life

Deacons are expected to participate actively in all aspects of the spiritual life of the church. If deacons do not have time for prayer meetings, Sunday morning worship, Bible studies, and the ministry of caring for the needs of the congregation during times of sickness or other distress, they should be removed from the board in favor of someone who wants to be involved in this important ministry.

Plenty of Ministry to Be Done!

The duties listed above include a wide range of important roles and responsibilities through which deacons serve their congregation. Deacons are involved in worship, Christian education, evangelism, new member orientation, oversight of benevolence work, screening new church leaders, and engagement with sister congregations during joint worship services. Along with other church leaders and the congregation as a whole, deacons share the responsibility for determining church policies and programs. Deacons play a key role during the ordinances of baptism and the Lord's Supper. They also represent the congregation at funerals as well as when they visit members at their homes or in the hospital.

Most of all, deacons support everything that goes on in the life of a congregation through what is known as the "ministry of presence." In many of these instances, they do not need to say or do anything. Their presence at the event is a much-appreciated sign of support for those who are sponsoring and participating in whatever is going on at the church at any given time.

These are the tasks that constitute "waiting on tables" for deacons in black Baptist churches of the twenty-first century. When these tasks are taken seriously, deacons will not be focused on what the pastor or other church auxiliaries are doing because, as the old spiritual says, "It takes all of my time to serve my Jesus, all of my time to serve the Lord." By the same token, these deacons play a role in our churches that is far too critical for them to be reduced to "armor bearers" for preachers more interested in having personal servants than in collaborating with partners in ministry who join the clergy in serving the needs of the congregation.

Notes

1. In addition to twenty pastors from Cleveland and twelve pastors from San Antonio's Community Churches for Social Action, the following clergy were surveyed: J. Alfred Smith Sr. from Oakland, CA; Wilma Johnson from Detroit, MI; Wayne Croft from Philadelphia, PA; James Perkins from Detroit, MI; Quincy Fortson from Elberton, GA; Alice Green from Chicago, IL; James Henry Harris from Richmond, VA; Marion Franklin from Vaux Hall, NJ; Thurman Walker from San Antonio, TX; George Gaymon from Columbia, SC; Jason Taylor from New Haven, CT; and Derrick Harkins from Washington, DC.

2. Respondents included pastors of churches belonging to the following Baptist denominations: National Baptist Convention USA, Inc., National Baptist Convention of America, Progressive National Baptist Convention, Full Gospel Baptist Church Fellowship, General Missionary Baptist Convention, Primitive Baptists of America, and American Baptist Churches USA.

Chapter 8

Profiles in Service

Our study of the role and responsibilities of the deacon in the black Baptist church concludes with a series of profiles that offer insight into the diversity of backgrounds and experiences present on deacon boards in black Baptist churches across the country. What will also be demonstrated is that despite the diversity present among those profiled, they all share a similar understanding of the role and responsibilities of the office of deacon. Each of these individuals is an exemplary deacon who embodies the characteristics of Acts 6:1-7 and 1 Timothy 3: 8-13. Every church would be blessed by the service of such persons.

Clifford Downer

The first person to be profiled is Clifford Downer who served as chairman of the board of deacons at Mt. Calvary Baptist Church in Elberton, Georgia, from the mid 1940s until his death in 1969. Born in Georgia in 1892, Clifford Downer was the embodiment of a generation of black men who had access to very few positions of leadership or influence outside of their local church. In addition to being a custodian at the all-white high school in Elberton, he was also the gardener and landscaper who maintained the lawn and flowers in the city square. Day in and day out Downer would encounter white men half his age who would address him as "Cliff," while he had to be careful to address those same men who were half his age as "Mister." On one occasion Clifford Downer was confronted by a white child less than ten years old who said to him, "Clifford, you ain't nothing but a dirty, black nigger." There was nothing Clifford Downer could say to rebuke that child, since it might have led to an even harsher confrontation with the parents of that youth or, more likely, with the official or even "unofficial" enforcers of white supremacy in that small southern town.

At the center of that city square in Elberton stands a towering white monument erected in honor of the soldiers from Elbert County, Georgia, who died in the service of the Confederate army during the Civil War. A black man named Clifford Downer maintained this public space that was set aside to honor men who had fought and died to keep his ancestors and their off-spring in slavery. On most workdays he was dressed in overalls despite the stifling heat of Georgia. Although he was beloved by his family and friends, he was largely ignored, overlooked, or disregarded by the white people who passed him as he maintained the city square and its monument.

At the end of each workday he returned to his modest wood-framed home on a dead-end street in the all-black section of that segregated Southern town. There were no prospects for his advancement within the municipal workforce of Elberton. There were no stores in downtown Elberton that would hire him to do anything other than another form of manual labor. Elberton refused to comply with the desegregation mandate of the 1954 *Brown v. Board of Education* decision until 1978. When the town finally did agree to end the practice of maintaining two separate and totally unequal school systems, they did not call it "desegregation." Instead, to avoid acknowledging that they had ever done anything wrong or unfair, they decided on a system of "consolidation" in which the formerly all-black schools were closed due to claims that it had become more "cost-effective" to maintain one unified school district. Of course, the impact of consolidation was that most of the black employees of the formerly all-black schools that were closed were left without jobs.

The Elberton in which Clifford Downer lived and worked was a town where a white man came to the home of a black family and urged the woman of the house to tell her husband to stop "talking back to white folks." The white man complained that, "He talks to me like he's the white man and I'm the nigger." Clearly, this was a community where no black man, no matter how old and no matter how hard-working, could expect to be viewed with respect or entrusted with power or influence.

However, in the language of Duke Ellington,[1] "Come Sunday," "Cliff" became Deacon Downer. The work shoes and overalls were replaced by a black suit with a crisp white handkerchief in the outside breast pocket of the jacket. Mt. Calvary had an itinerant pastor who was present at the church two Sundays each month. On the other Sundays the deacons would be in charge of the church and would preside at Sunday school and other church functions. That meant that Deacon Downer essentially ran the church most of the time. He was a constant source of leadership and stability for a congregation that only saw its pastor for a few hours each month. One hundred years of both the joys and sorrows of black history were wrapped up in the life of Clifford Downer both inside and outside his church in Georgia.

It is important to report that when the pastor was away at other churches Deacon Downer never sought to undermine the pastor. On those Sundays when the pastor was present Deacon Downer never failed to relinquish primary authority over the church to that pastor for as long as he was among them. Circumstances required that Deacon Downer fill a leadership position, but Christian character allowed him to lead with a servant's heart. He kept the church focused on its mission and ministry in that community and was never accused of using his role as chairman of the deacon board to promote himself or put down the pastor. He was a good example of what it means to be a *diakonos*—one who waits on tables in order to meet the needs of the people in the church.

Jimmy Noble

The next deacon to be profiled is Jimmy Noble, who happens to be the grandson of Clifford Downer. Like his grandfather, Jimmy Noble was born and raised in Elberton, Georgia. After completing high school, he went on to graduate from Savannah State University (GA) in 1975 with a degree in criminal justice. He immediately began a career in law enforcement, serving first as a deputy sheriff in Silver Springs, Maryland. In 1982 he became a police officer with the Athens-Clarke County Sheriff's Office in Georgia. Now in his thirty-fifth year in law enforcement, Jimmy Noble has served in the Athens, Georgia, area as chief investigator with the state solicitor's office, which is the office of the state's prosecuting attorney. He was chief marshal with Athens-Clarke County from 1997–2004, and now serves as a code enforcement officer for Athens-Clarke County.

In 1985 Jimmy Noble was first ordained as a deacon by the Mt. Calvary Baptist Church of Elberton—the same church where he had been raised and where his grandfather had served as chairman of the deacon board for so many years. In 2000 he was ordained again to serve as a deacon at St. Timothy Baptist Church in Athens, Georgia. The world changed drastically from the time of Clifford Downer to the time of Jimmy Noble. One never finished high school and the other one graduated from college. One was confined to a world of janitorial and custodial work, while the other one has spent his career as a law enforcement official complete with a gun, a badge, and the power to put black and white people in jail. One lived in the segregated section of Elberton in the days of Jim Crow, while the other one lives in a towering brick home in an exclusive development in an affluent suburb of Athens where most of his neighbors are white including the head football coach of the University of Georgia.

Clifford Downer's wife, Annie Lee Downer, worked primarily in food service in the local hospital. Jimmy Noble's wife, Martha Noble, has an Ed.D. from Georgia Southern University and serves as director of human resources for the public schools of Elberton, Georgia—the same town that delayed its compliance with the 1954 *Brown* decision for almost a quarter of a century. In fact, Martha Noble now works in a building that, forty years earlier, was an all-white middle school that her eventual husband had not been permitted to attend, even though it stood less than two hundred feet from his back door.

Despite the status Jimmy Noble enjoys as a law enforcement official and the authority he exercises every day over blacks and whites, he too has a "Come Sunday" transformation. As a deacon, Jimmy Noble willingly seeks out whatever service he can offer to his church family. He assists in serving meals at the church. He supports the pastor during revivals and other special programs. He does not try to remind anybody that he is "the law." Instead, he embodies a spirit of humility, service, and generosity. The world in which he lives is fundamentally transformed beyond anything his grandfather could have imagined. Nevertheless, these two men approached their role and responsibilities as a deacon in exactly the same way. They are *diakonoi*—servants of God who wait on tables and serve the needs of the congregation. When asked the primary role of a deacon, Jimmy Noble answers by saying, "Deacons should assist the pastor in serving the church in every way possible."

Four Deacons Named Brown

The next four deacons to be profiled all share the same last name—Brown. The first three of these deacons all serve at Antioch Baptist Church in Cleveland, where I have been pastor for more than two decades. They have been selected for attention here not because they serve more effectively than the other deacons of the church. Instead, they have been chosen because of the many fascinating contrasts between them that point to the diversity of people who are willing and able to serve in the life of their church as deacons. The deacons in question are Leroy Brown, Tilmon Brown, and Delores Brown—and three more faithful deacons cannot be found! The fourth deacon to be profiled here is John Brown, chairman of the deacon board at First Baptist Church in Vaux Hall, New Jersey. While he and I never served together in the same congregation, I was privileged to be the preacher for his ordination service in 1979.

Leroy Brown

Leroy Brown has served as a deacon at Antioch Baptist Church since 1969, and has been chairman of the board of deacons at Antioch since 1985. He was born in Hall County, Georgia, in 1922, and spent his youth working as a sharecropper as was the expectation of young black children in Georgia at that time. As a teenager he secured a job as a waiter at the Atlanta Athletic Club before enlisting in the US Navy at the age of 18. In accordance with the policies of a segregated navy, he served as chief of the stewards (cooks and custodians) aboard a ship assigned to the Pacific Ocean during World War II. Even stewards had battle stations during times of combat, and Leroy Brown's job was to load ammunition on a conveyor belt that was carried to the big guns on the deck of the ship. He once told me that "Praise the Lord and pass the ammunition" was his theme song. The most famous ship's steward during World War II was Dorie Miller, who won the Navy Cross for shooting down four Japanese planes during the attack on Pearl Harbor on December 7, 1941.

Leroy Brown and his wife, Lillie, migrated to Cleveland in 1946, and soon joined the Antioch Baptist Church. He quickly found out that racism was not confined to southern states. In fact, he reports that the racism he experienced in Cleveland was worse than anything he had encountered in Georgia. There were a host of jobs unavailable to him solely because he was black, even though he was a returning war veteran. Like thousands of other black people, he was finally able to secure steady employment in the auto industry.

After beginning as a custodian at General Motors in 1948, he worked on the production line from 1950 to 1971. Finally, he was allowed to take the test that enabled him to attain a skilled position working as an electrician. He spent a total of forty-five years working for General Motors in the Fisher Body division. Just as the story of racism in the Deep South could be told through the experiences of Clifford Downer, the struggles of black people who were a part of the Great Migration could be told through the experiences of Leroy Brown.

"Come Sunday" everything changed for this black man. Antioch Baptist Church has long been a pillar in Cleveland's black community, and Leroy Brown has chaired its board of deacons for twenty-five years. The black church has created a level playing field where someone with only a high school diploma could lead a group of deacons comprised of professionals from every walk of life. It is fascinating to watch corporate and nonprofit executives, lawyers, bankers, educators, and small business entrepreneurs honor and affirm the leadership of this former sharecropper. There are few, if any, places outside of the black church where such an arrangement could even be imagined, much less observed.

Leroy Brown knows what it is like to serve as a *diakonos* at a time when the church was without a pastor. The pastor of Antioch Baptist Church from 1964 to 1983 was Emmanuel Branche. This Yale College and Yale Divinity School graduate died during the winter of 1983, leaving the church without a pastor until my arrival in the fall of 1986. During that time, Leroy Brown was the leader of the congregation. It was a challenging time for the congregation and quite a test of his leadership skills, but by all accounts Deacon Leroy Brown served with distinction. He oversaw the selection of preachers from week to week, moderated church meetings, and served as chairman of the pastoral search committee. He excelled in all those assignments, gaining the admiration and respect of the entire congregation.

When I was installed as the new pastor in February of 1987, Leroy Brown offered essential and loyal support to me in my new role. He continues to attend every worship service, participates in a Sunday school class, attends almost every special event at the church, and is part of all outside trips—whether to worship with another congregation, to share with inmates in the chapel at one of Ohio's prisons, or to support the pastor during various ecumenical and interfaith activities. In addition to that, he joins a group of three other deacons and one deacon's wife in overseeing the benevolence work of the church, assisting both members and non-members with food, utility bills, prescription medicine costs, and other moderately priced emergency needs. At the age of 85, he continues to make hospital and home visits, to attend nearly every funeral held at the church, to consult with the pastor before every Sunday morning service, and to preside at the monthly meetings of the board of deacons. Leroy Brown is a *diakonos* who serves the people by practicing the modern forms of waiting on tables. He describes deacons as "the spiritual leaders of the church whose primary task is to assist the pastor in any way possible."

Tilmon Brown

Tilmon Brown's life experiences offer a sharp contrast to those of Leroy Brown. These two men serve on the same deacon board, but that is where the similarities between them end. While Leroy Brown was born in segregated Georgia prior to the Great Depression and served in World War II, Tilmon Brown was born in Buffalo, New York, in 1945, and was part of the first wave of baby-boomers born after World War II. A graduate of the State University of New York in Buffalo, he got an early start in the retail sales business with the Continental Baking Company. He worked with that company from 1966 to 1995, following the usual corporate pattern of moving from one city to another as his career path developed. His job took him to Rochester, New York; Atlanta, Georgia; Montclair, New Jersey; Stamford, Connecticut; and St. Louis, Missouri.

After thirty years with the Continental Baking Company, he launched out into a new career. In 1995 he became a partner of the New Horizons Baking Company, which he now owns. For several years this multimillion-dollar company located in Norwalk, Ohio, has been listed among *Black Enterprise* magazine's top one hundred black-owned businesses in the US. The company has a multi-racial workforce of over 200 persons that bake and deliver the buns and other bread products for all of the McDonald's restaurants in a seven-state region surrounding Ohio. His business skill and acumen was recognized and tapped when he was recently appointed to a seat on the board of the Federal Reserve Bank of Cleveland, which is the fourth of the twelve Federal Reserve Bank districts of the United States. His business and management skills are also called upon in his role as a member of the board of trustees of Ashland Theological Seminary in Ohio.

Tilmon Brown got an early start as a deacon in the black Baptist church. He was first ordained at the St. John Baptist Church of Buffalo in 1968 at the age of 23. Shortly after a corporate move took him to Connecticut, he was ordained as a deacon by the Union Baptist Church of Stamford in 1985. After moving to Ohio to own and operate his own business, he joined the Antioch Baptist Church, where he was ordained as a deacon for a third time in 1998.

"Come Sunday" has a very different meaning for Tilmon Brown than it ever did for Clifford Downer or Leroy Brown. Sunday is an opportunity for him to publicly give thanks to the God who has "opened the windows of heaven and poured out a blessing that there is not room enough to receive" (Malachi 3:10). Despite his crowded schedule and great responsibilities as a business owner, he is a dedicated and devoted member of the deacon board. He and his wife, Jonnie, drive from a great distance to be present in church every Sunday. They both sing in one of the church choirs, and he is regularly featured as a soloist.

He maintains active contact with the twenty-five members of the church assigned to him as their shepherding deacon.

Tilmon Brown has been willing to serve the church in ways that are unique to a man in his position. On more than a few occasions I have been able to arrange for him to meet with members of the church who needed business and financial advice that was beyond my scope of knowledge or ability but was right up his alley. He has been willing to counsel people about all aspects of their personal and business finances. Along with three other deacons of the church—all of whom come from the business or corporate world—he serves on the board of our church's nonprofit community development corporation. Their collective wisdom and insight has been invaluable as they have served the church through that particular vehicle. Much of Antioch Baptist Church's community outreach ministry is funded by and performed through our CDC, and it has been another way that people with the right skills can "wait on tables" and serve the needs of the church. When asked to sum up his understanding of the role of a deacon, he turns to the language of Acts 6:3, saying, "I want to be a man who is full of the Holy Spirit and wisdom who strives to serve the people of God."

Delores Brown

The next person to be profiled in this study is Delores Brown, a native of Jackson, Mississippi, who was ordained as a deacon at Antioch Baptist Church in 1998. Since then, she has been something of a trailblazer while serving in a position that had been limited to men from the formation of Antioch in 1893 until the first woman deacon was ordained in 1997. Delores Brown was a teacher for twenty-four years in the Cleveland Public School system. Throughout those years she was actively involved in the church, serving as a Sunday school teacher and the director of the Vacation Bible School, as well as being actively involved in the various women's ministry projects of the church. Up until her ordination as a deacon, one could say that she faithfully conformed to the roles that were expected of or available to women in the black Baptist church for the last one hundred years.

Very few people are ever elevated to the position of deacon in the black Baptist church. Most men who are approached about becoming a deacon typically view it as a great honor, and most are quick to embrace the opportunity even though they know that a great deal of service waits on the other side of ordination. When a woman is approached about accepting an appointment to the deacon board of a black Baptist church, there is even more that she must consider. How will the congregation respond to a woman deacon? Even if her own congregation is fully supportive, what will happen if her church is invited to worship with another congregation, and the visiting deacons are invited to come forward and help lead the devotional service? Will she be welcomed or excluded from that role? What will her husband and her children think about her moving into a position that has always been understood as reserved for the men in the church?

Male candidates for deacon in the black church are, in many ways, like white candidates for a job in the wider society, in that there are some restrictions and limitations that never even cross their minds. Male privilege, like white privilege, often remains unspoken until someone from outside that privileged group tries to move into the neighborhood. Then the walls and biases appear as quickly in one setting as they do in the other. Delores Brown and the other six women who serve on our deacon board had to contend with more than the time commitment involved in becoming a deacon. They all had to contend with the centuries-long practice of women being told that the Bible prohibited them from serving in that position. Indeed, Delores Brown was told exactly that by certain individuals recently when she visited her home state of Mississippi. The courage required of a woman seeking to integrate the all-male deacon board of a black Baptist church in the 1990s was not unlike what was demanded of those black young people seeking to integrate all-white universities and high schools in the 1950s and 1960s. While these churchwomen did not encounter racism coupled with violence, they did confront sexism coupled with scorn—some of which came from other women in the church.

As with Tilmon Brown, "waiting on tables" has taken on a special meaning for Delores Brown due to her unique position and experience. Since we made the decision to begin ordaining women as deacons in our church, several other black Baptist churches in Cleveland have taken a similar step. One of those churches asked us to provide a female deacon from our church who could serve as a mentor and encourager for the woman they were about to ordain in their church. It was Delores Brown who agreed to serve in that capacity, and for many months she talked and prayed with her sister until that woman felt secure in her new position. Her experience as a woman deacon made her uniquely equipped to serve in this way.

In 2009 *The African American Pulpit* asked me to identify a deacon who might write an article for its online lectionary service. They were seeking someone who could offer a lesson focused on the role of the deacon that could also be used as a guideline for services of ordination of deacons in local churches across the country. Given her twenty-four years as an educator and her eleven years of experience as a deacon, Delores Brown was the perfect choice. Her careful analysis of 1 Timothy 3:8-13, her recollections of her own ordination service, and her clear understanding of the role and responsibilities of deacons in the black Baptist church came shining through in that essay.[2] Asked to define the work of a deacon, she states, "Deacons work with the pastor to meet the physical, emotional, and spiritual needs of the congregation and the community." This is perfectly in line with what Acts 6:1-7 had in mind.

John Brown

The experience of John Brown includes involvement in a South Carolina church with an itinerant minister, as well as service as chairman of the board in a church going through a time of great conflict. Brown was born in Rock Hill, South Carolina, in 1938. His own parents were not active in the church, so he owes his early religious upbringing to neighbors who would take him along when they went to church.

The Nazarene Baptist Church in Rock Hill had an itinerant pastor who was present only once a month. However, instead of the deacons handling morning worship on other Sundays, this church was unique in that most members of Nazarene would simply attend worship at whatever church their pastor was serving each Sunday. The deacons did lead in other ways; John's earliest memories of the black Baptist church involve deacons leading the congregation in the singing of long-meter hymns where standard songs from the hymnal were movingly transformed into the slower and more punctuated rhythms associated with black Baptist worship in the nineteenth and early twentieth centuries. None of the churches in Rock Hill had any instruments, so the voices of the deacons became the center of the worship experience.

John relocated to New Jersey in 1959 and began working as a custodian in a tool-and-die company. He then qualified to become a machinist—a profession he continued in until he became a barber in 1975. In 1963 he joined Messiah Baptist Church in East Orange, New Jersey, where he experienced his first real spiritual awakening. In 1968 he became a deacon in that church and served in that role until 1975. After he and his family relocated to Maplewood, New Jersey, John left Messiah to join First Baptist Church of Vaux Hall, New Jersey. In the black Baptist tradition, one's status as a deacon with one congregation does not automatically transfer to another congregation, but after several years in that congregation, John was invited to become a deacon there in 1979. John had to be ordained again into service as a deacon in this church, and I had the privilege of preaching the ordination sermon at that service by invitation of Dr. Marion Franklin, one of the pastors who was interviewed for this study.

John Brown became chair of the deacon board at First Baptist Church in 1991, and that is when his trial by fire occurred. Some deacons in that church charged the pastor and the church treasurer with misappropriation of funds. With a firm belief that these charges were false and inappropriate, John Brown refused to join with other deacons in this action, arguing that the deacons were behaving improperly. The other deacons accused John of being a "pastor lover," to which he proudly responded, "I am."

Several deacons sought to bring a legal action against the pastor, but a local court refused to hear the case and urged the church to work things out internally. After the judge referred the matter back to the church, some of the deacons who had brought the charge against the pastor left the church. Those who did not leave voluntarily were voted off the board by the congregation. The only deacon who remained after the conflict was John Brown. He stated his belief that nothing improper had been done by the pastor or treasurer and, moreover, that he saw nothing in Scripture that justified what the deacons on his board were doing. He was not going to join them in doing what was wrong.

There may be times when legitimate issues of misconduct within the church do exist, and there may be some need for deacons to be involved. At such a time, the church by-laws and/or constitution should always provide guidance. It is the role and purpose of openly announced church meetings to air such issues in the presence of any and all members that are free to attend. Confidential issues can and should be resolved by the use of the biblical model in Matthew 18:15-17. However, neither deacons, trustees, or any other officer or member in the church should conduct secret meetings in order to carry out church business!

When asked to describe the work of a deacon, John Brown said, "Deacons should be committed to Jesus Christ and should walk circumspectly under the guidance of the Holy Spirit. They should support the vision of the pastor, and when they cannot support that vision, they should step aside and not block the progress of the church."

George Gaymon

The final profile in this study is in some respects the most interesting and revealing of them all, for it is the story of a "twenty-first century Stephen." George Gaymon served as a church deacon for many years, working closely with the pastor. Eventually, he was called into pastoral ministry himself, and had the opposite experience of having to work with deacons as a pastor. George Gaymon was ordained to be a deacon at St. Paul Baptist Church in Montclair, New Jersey, in 1980, during my tenure as pastor of that congregation. He served that church as a deacon until 1989, and on two separate occasions served a three-year term as chairman of the deacon board. It was while serving as a deacon that he experienced a call into the pastoral ministry and was later licensed by the same church that had ordained him to be a deacon. Like Stephen and Philip who were set apart as deacons in Acts 6:1-6 but then moved beyond that initial calling to work as evangelists, George Gaymon represents those hundreds of deacons in black Baptist churches across the country who answer a subsequent call to the pastoral ministry and begin to preach the gospel.

George Gaymon was born in Panola, South Carolina, in 1939. After serving in the United States Air Force from 1963–1971, he took a job as an administrator at Harlem Hospital in New York City. He and his family relocated to Montclair, New Jersey, in 1973, where he earned an undergraduate degree from Montclair State University in 1978. He went on to earn an MBA at Fairleigh Dickinson University in 1980, the same year he became an administrator with the University of Medicine and Dentistry of New Jersey. Ten years later, in 1990 he returned to his native state of South Carolina, where he began working for the state in the department of durable medical equipment. It was after his return to South Carolina that his transition from deacon to preacher took final form.

In 1991 George Gaymon was called as pastor of Old Wilson Baptist Church in Chester, South Carolina. It was there that he was ordained into the pastoral ministry. He had begun his training for the ministry a few years earlier at Drew University School of Theology in Madison, New Jersey, and earned his Master of Divinity in 1992 from Faith Baptist Seminary in Anderson, South Carolina, and a Doctor of Divinity from the same school the next year. He continues to pursue a Doctor of Ministry from Trinity Theological Seminary of Newburgh, Indiana.

From 1993 to 2004 he served as pastor of Rehoboth Baptist Church in Columbia, South Carolina. During that period the church grew from 50 members to more than 500 members and added a family life center as well as daycare and afterschool care programs. It was while serving this church that George Gaymon found himself, a former deacon, in conflict with his own deacon board. When the deacons of that church thought he was doing too much too soon and leading the church into areas of ministry that were new to them, they orchestrated his removal from his position as pastor. In a meeting that ran from 7:00 PM until 3:00 the next morning, persons who were on the church rolls but who had never attended church since he had been there as pastor turned out to cast votes to remove him from his position. After his sudden dismissal from that church, he led in the organization of a new church that was founded in November 2004—New Revelation Baptist Church of Blythewood, South Carolina. Today, that congregation is poised to start a building program for a new church home.

This former deacon's experiences have left him with a keen sense of how quickly deacons can cross the line from assisting the pastor to running the pastor and sometimes even ruining the church. In commenting on his experiences in 2004, he stated, "Deacons have a tendency to believe they and not God own the church." The majority of the deacons who voted to remove him as pastor had been serving for at least thirty years. It was generally assumed that deacons in that church would serve in their positions for life, and clergy were seen as nonessential employees. After all, it was the deacons who were the constant fixture in the life of that congregation. However, those deacons did not operate out of an Acts 6:1-7 or 1 Timothy 3:8-13 model. This was a clear example of the deacons operating as a board of directors that hires and fires church employees, while the deacons themselves are not subjected to any outside scrutiny or accountability. This was exactly the kind of action that John Brown of First Baptist Church in Vaux Hall, New Jersey, refused to allow.

Looking through his unique lens as both a pastor and a former deacon, George Gaymon contends that the role of the deacons in a black Baptist church is to support the pastor who has received a vision from God, and then assist in carrying out that vision. That is a far cry from what happened to him when he was cast out of his church in a deacon-led revolt, ostensibly for ministry work that moved too far too fast. Like Stephen from the Book of Acts, George Gaymon was attacked by the very people he sought to lead and serve. This episode is a fresh reminder that the problem of "bossism" is alive and well among some deacons in the black Baptist church. Despite this negative personal experience, Gaymon continue to believe that, "deacons hold a very important position and play a useful role in the life of the church."

A Concluding Thought

Deacons of the twenty-first century black Baptist church serve in a vastly different world from that of the early Christian church in which the office of deacon was initially conceived and created. We have seen this true so far especially as the role and status of women is concerned. It has been argued here and elsewhere that, just as the role and status of women in society has dramatically changed in the last two thousand years, their role and status in the life of the black Baptist church cannot remain frozen by the cultural assumptions of the first century. It is an act of bad faith to take a literal reading of passages such as 1 Corinthians 14:33-35 or 1 Timothy 2:11-13 and assume that a direct application of those instructions is appropriate for the church of today. We must recognize the way in which the second-class status of women in the first century directly informed the language of those biblical texts now being used by those who oppose women in leadership roles in the church today.

That being said, the essential purpose and role of deacons in the church has not changed from the time of the early church in Jerusalem to today; nor should it ever change. Deacons, both then and now, are called to a ministry of service in the local church. When they serve in that role the church is likely to be blessed and to greatly benefit from their service. When deacons depart from that role of service and "waiting on tables," choosing instead to try to run the pastor and the church themselves, the seeds are sown for conflict that can cause the work of the ministry to be frustrated and obscured by contentious power struggles.

Beginning with seven men in the church in Jerusalem and extending to the men and women serving in black Baptist churches throughout the United States today, the ministry of deacons is essential to the effective work of the church of Jesus Christ. But that work must be done with and in the right spirit. There is always a need for more *diakonoi* who will serve the needs of the congregations. However, deacons must remember that the office should not be manipulated to hold prominence over the people or to exercise authority over the pastor. Such an approach is, as we have clearly seen, contrary to what the biblical models set forth.

At the same time, pastors need to understand that they, too, are called to serve the Lord and serve the church. In an age of celebrity preachers who fly on private jets, drive Bentley automobiles, and surround themselves with "armor bearers" on every side, pastors must never turn their position from a role of serving the church into an opportunity to focus on being served by others. When black Baptist churches unite around this concept of servant leadership by both ordained offices—preachers and deacons—they might become like the early Christian community in Jerusalem in the aftermath of the Day of Pentecost who were known for "praising God and enjoying the favor of all the people. And the Lord added to their number daily those who were being saved" (Acts 2:47, NIV).

Notes

1. Edward "Duke" Ellington, "Come Sunday," from The First Sacred Concert presented at Grace Cathedral in San Francisco, CA, on September 16, 1965.
2. Delores Brown, "An Ordination of New Deacons," *The African American Pulpit Lectionary,* March 7, 2010.

°Appendix A°
Questionnaire about the Role of Deacons in the Black Baptist Church

Please answer each of these questions with a yes or no response.

How does someone become a deacon?

1. Does your church have a board of deacons? _____
2. Are the deacons in your church elected by a vote of the congregation? _____
3. Are deacons in your church directly appointed by the pastor? _____
4. Do deacons in your church serve lifetime appointments? _____
5. Do deacons in your church have to be periodically reelected to terms of service? _____
6. Are deacons in your church required to rotate off the board after a certain number of years? _____
7. Does your church screen deacons according to Acts 6:1-7 or 1 Timothy 3:8-13? _____
8. Are deacons in your church ordained in a public ceremony with laying on of hands? _____
9. Do existing deacons screen or approve all persons being considered to become a deacon? _____
10. Must a person serve in other positions before they can become a deacon in your church? _____

Who can become a deacon?

1. Can an unmarried person become a deacon in your church? _____

2. Can a person who has been divorced become a deacon, in your church? _____

3. If a person gets a divorce after becoming a deacon can they remain on your deacon board? _____

4. Can a woman serve on your deacon board? _____

5. Are women currently serving as deacons in your church?

    _____

6. Can persons under the age of 21 serve as deacons in your church? _____

7. Can an openly gay or lesbian person serve as a deacon in your church? _____

8. Can a non-African American serve as a deacon in your church? _____

9. Can a recent convert to Christianity (5 years or less) be a deacon in your church? _____

10. Can anyone with a known criminal record serve as a deacon in your church? _____

What is the role of the deacon?

1. Do deacons serve as primary worship leaders in your church? _____

2. Are deacons required to make home and hospital visits to your sick and shut-in members? _____

3. Are deacons expected to be active in Sunday school and/or some other Bible study? _____

4. Are deacons allowed to serve on other church auxiliaries (choirs, etc.)? _____

5. Do deacons in your church assist in serving Communion?

6. Do deacons in your church assist in preparing candidates for baptism? _____

7. Do deacons in your church assist in the orientation of new members in your church? _____

8. Do deacons in your church screen and aid in the selection of other church officers? _____

9. Do deacons in your church play any role in overseeing church finances? _____

10. Do deacons join in extending the right hand of fellowship to new members of your church? _____

What is the relationship between the deacons and the pastor?

1. Does the pastor meet with the deacons on a regular basis? _____

2. Do the pastor and deacons often find themselves in disagreement over church policy? _____

3. Do the deacons sponsor an annual appreciation day for the work of the pastor? _____

4. Does the pastor publicly commend the work being done by the deacons? _____

5. Has the pastor at your church ever disapproved someone who had been recommended to be a deacon? _____

6. Has the pastor ever asked a deacon to leave the board for any reason? _____

7. Have the deacons in your church ever brought charges for dismissal or discipline against the pastor? _____

8. Has the pastor of your church ever disbanded, or sought to disband the deacon board in favor of some other form of lay leadership? _____

9. Do deacons in your church meet with the pastor before each Sunday service for prayer? _____

10. Does the pastor meet with and pre-approve anyone who is being recommended to the deacon board? _____

Results of the Questionnaire about the Role of Deacons in the Black Baptist Church

How does someone become a deacon?

1. 41 of the 44 churches responding to the survey have persons who serve as deacons.
2. 39 of the 44 churches elect their deacons by a vote of the congregation.
3. 5 churches allow the pastor to appoint deacons.
4. 33 churches allow deacons to serve for life.
5. 11 churches require deacons to be reelected periodically.
6. 10 churches require deacons to rotate off the board after a set number of years.
7. 40 churches state they use Acts 6:1-7 and 1 Timothy 3:8-13 in their process of screening new deacons.
8. 40 churches ordain deacons through the laying on of hands.
9. 36 churches allow existing deacons to share in the screening process for persons being considered to become new deacons.
10. 38 churches require a person to serve in another leadership position in that church before they can become a deacon.

Who can become a deacon?

1. 39 churches allow an unmarried person to serve as a deacon.

2. 41 churches allow a divorced person to serve as a deacon.
3. 39 churches allow a person who gets a divorce while serving as a deacon to remain in that position.
4. 21 churches do not prohibit women from serving as deacons.
5. 7 churches have at least one woman currently serving as a deacon, and in one church a woman serves as chairman of the deacon board.
6. 4 churches would allow someone under the age of 21 to serve as a deacon.
7. Only one church in the survey would allow an openly gay or lesbian person to serve as a deacon.
8. 37 churches would allow a non-African American to serve as a deacon.
9. 33 churches would allow a recent convert of less than 5 years to serve as a deacon.
10. 39 churches would allow someone with a criminal record to serve as a deacon.

What is the role of the deacon?

1. 28 churches use deacons as their primary worship leaders.
2. All 44 churches expect deacons to make sick visits to members in their homes and at hospitals.
3. 42 churches expect deacons to be involved in some form of Christian education.
4. 42 churches allow deacons to serve with other church auxiliaries.
5. All 44 churches involve deacons in serving the Lord's Supper.
6. All 44 churches involve deacons in the ordinance of baptism.
7. 37 churches involve deacons in new member orientation.
8. 35 churches involve deacons in screening other church-wide officers.
9. Only 6 churches involve deacons in handling the finances of the church.

10. All 44 churches involve deacons in extending the right hand of fellowship to new members of the church.

What is the relationship between the deacons and the pastor?

1. In 38 churches the pastor meets with the deacons on a regular basis.
2. In 16 churches the pastor and deacons regularly disagree over church policy.
3. In 28 churches deacons sponsor an annual appreciation day for the pastor.
4. In 39 churches the pastor regularly and publicly commends the deacons for their work.
5. In 33 of the churches the pastor has blocked someone who had been recommended to become a deacon.
6. In 32 churches the pastor dismissed a deacon from the board for various reasons.
7. In 7 churches the deacons brought morals or malfeasance charges against the pastor.
8. In 7 of the churches the pastor has disbanded the entire board of deacons in favor of another form of lay leadership.
9. In 35 churches the pastor and deacons pray together prior to every worship service.
10. In 42 churches the pastor pre-approves anyone who serves as a deacon.